D1761699

Economics-Based Writing Lessons

in Structure & Style

by
Daniel K. Weber

Student Book

First Edition © January 2010
Institute for Excellence in Writing, L.L.C.

Also by Daniel K. Weber:

Character-Based Writing Lessons

The purchase of this book entitles its owner to a free downloadable copy of *The Student Resource Notebook.*
Go to: www.excellenceinwriting.com/EBW-E

Copyright Policy

Institute for Excellence in Writing
8799 N. 387 Road
Locust Grove, OK 74352
800.856.5815
info@excellenceinwriting.com
www.excellenceinwriting.com

Printed in the United States of America

Accessing Your Download

The purchase of this book entitles its owner to a free download of the optional *Student Resource Notebook e-book* (110 pages*).

To download your complimentary e-book, please follow the directions below:

1. Go to our website, excellenceinwriting.com
2. Sign in to your online customer account. If you do not have an account, you will need to create one.
3. After you are logged in, go to this web page: excellenceinwriting.com/EBW-E
4. Click on the red download arrow.
5. You will be taken to your File Downloads page. Click on the file name, and the e-book will download onto your computer.

Please note: You are free to download and print this e-book resource as many times as needed for use within *your immediate family or classroom*. However, this information is proprietary, and we are trusting you to be on your honor not to share it with anyone. Please see the copyright page for further details. Thank you.

*If you would prefer to purchase the *Student Resource Notebook* as a preprinted, spiral-bound book, it is available at excellenceinwriting.com/SRN-B

If you have any difficulty receiving this download after going through the steps above, please call 800.856.5815.

Institute for Excellence in Writing
8799 N. 387 Road
Locust Grove, OK 74352

Contents

Acknowledgement

My dear friend, Andrew Pudewa, provided support and guidance during the creation of this book. It is his foundational program for teaching writing upon which the lessons of this book are structured. I am grateful for Andrew's loving kindness, enthusiasm, vision, creativity, wisdom, and devotion.

To the Student...

Growing up, I always hated having people tell me what to do. I wanted to dream my own dreams and make those dreams come true. I always felt like I could stay one step ahead of everybody else. I was not afraid to take risks or to put in the hard work necessary to make things happen. I was always looking for opportunities, ready to seize the moment. I loved any big challenge and enjoyed overcoming an obstacle as much as the rewards that would inevitably follow. Like my grandfather always said, "Problems are opportunities in work clothes." It is always okay to fall down, but you've got to get back up, dust yourself off, and journey onward. Failure is only temporary, and it always provides an opportunity to learn. I hope you will learn a great deal from the lessons in this book.

These lessons are designed to help you think about entrepreneurial effort, business opportunity, innovation, creativity, and economic freedom. These lessons should also strengthen your composition skills. I have tried to select stories, excerpts, and historical references that are both interesting and important.

Almost every lesson has a source text for you to read before you start your assignments. After you have read the source text for a given lesson, please do the assignments in the order they appear. Each lesson builds upon the previous ones, as the checksheets clearly show. The checksheets are meant as guides – use them to remind yourself of the skills you have already learned and to make sure you have incorporated new skills into your compositions.

Spaces for your outlines are provided throughout, however, it may be more convenient to use a separate sheet of paper. This will eliminate the hassle of flipping back and forth from the source text to your outline as you work along.

Some of the later lessons will seem to skip a step in the assignment section. For instance, the assignment may simply say to write a composition. However, by that time, you should already know the model and the process: You must still make a note outline, write at least two drafts, and keep your final composition in the back of this book, or in a special folder.

If something isn't clear, don't hesitate to ask your parent or teacher for help. Discuss each lesson with them. This is not meant to be a workbook that you use all by yourself; it is a book of lessons which should be used under the guidance of your parent or teacher.

To the Parent and Teacher...

This book is intended primarily for use with IEW's Teaching Writing: Structure and Style program. If you are not familiar with that course, you may find this book difficult to use. Along those lines, it is important to understand that this is not a workbook that will teach the student writing. It is a collection of lessons that you, the teacher, can use to teach writing. You are the critical element for success with this book.

You will notice that I have included a variety of source text material. These source texts are designed to introduce your students to the concept of "Freedomship." The term "Freedomship Education" was coined by Andrew Pudewa a few years ago. Here's the definition: "The act or process of imparting, acquiring, or developing the character, knowledge, and skills necessary for being or remaining free." Free societies endorse free business practices, innovation, and entrepreneurialism in order to assure a flourishing economy. At this time in history, perhaps more than ever before, we need to pay close attention to the Political-Economy surrounding us. We also need to equip our youth with the tools and skills required to understand and communicate about economics and its importance in maintaining freedom. Reading about economics and then writing about economics has the power to assist young minds in the formation and personalization of these tools and skills.

Different students require different levels of challenge. This book provides checksheets at three levels: Level A – beginner, Level B – intermediate, and Level C – advanced. Level A students progress through the lessons focusing on the fundamentals of style. Level B students are expected to learn the fundamentals and build upon these skills with more detail. Level C students should already be familiar with (or should quickly learn) the basics of the skills taught, have a firm grasp of grammar, and be able to employ the advanced techniques that are taught in this book. The checksheets for each lesson, however, are suggested. If your students work at a different pace, that's okay. The lessons aren't rigid. You should adjust the checksheet to include or exclude skills as you progress. The flexibility makes this an ideal book for teaching mixed grade groups.

Some of the punctuation or grammar taught in this book may differ slightly from what you have learned before or normally practice in your home or classroom. You are the teacher, and it is your prerogative to teach your students what you want them to learn. If, for example, you disagree with the absence of a comma before a particular "who/which" clause, put it in. If you believe firmly in using "because" instead of "since" (or vice versa), teach it. These lessons are not meant to be authoritative about grammar and usage, but to be a source of ideas, models, and techniques to broaden composition experience and aptitude.

As you may have noticed, the checksheets throughout the book do not have a section to assign grades. The model checksheet on the next page includes a grading system for those who wish to grade their students' compositions.

(Model) Graded Checksheet for Lesson 3

Levels A, B, & C

Presentation
___ title centered and underlined (2)
___ name, date (1)
___ clearly presented (1)

Mechanics
___ indent paragraphs (1)
___ complete sentences (2)
___ capitals (uppercase) (2)
___ punctuation (2)

Style Tools
___ underline dress-ups (one of each) (1)

Level A

Dress-Ups
"-ly" word   ___ (2)
"who/which" clause   ___ (2)

Level B

Dress-Ups
"-ly" word   ___ (2)
"who/which" clause   ___ (2)
no "to be" verbs with
"who/which" clause   ___ (2)

Level C

Dress-Ups
"-ly" word   ___ (2)
"who/which" clause   ___ (2)
invisible "who/which" clause ___ (2)
no "to be" verbs with
"who/which" clause   ___ (2)

	Style Point Totals	**Total Points**	**Your Grade**
Level A	___/4	___/16	A = 90% - 100%
Level B	___/6	___/18	B = 80% - 90% C = 70% - 80%
Level C	___/8	___/20	D = 60% - 70% F = 0% - 60%

If you wish to grade your students' writing, you may assign points to each of the items on the checksheet. To obtain grade percentages: divide the total number of points the student earns by the number of points possible. Then multiply by 100 to get the percentage. For example, if a Level B student received 5 style points and 15 points total, the percentage would be 83.33%, a B.

Unit I: Note Taking
Lesson 1: Economics Defined

Objective
To learn how to take notes in an outline format, using Roman numerals and Arabic numbers.

Source Text

To study economics is to study the production, allocation, and use of goods and services. It is important to study how resources are distributed in order to satisfy the needs of the greatest number of people for the "common good." As we are more connected globally, the study of economics becomes even more important.

The two major divisions within the study of economics are known as macroeconomics and microeconomics. Macroeconomics is the study of whole systems within a single country or multiple countries considering all global issues. Microeconomics is the study of how the systems affect a single business or industry.

Assignment
1. Read the source text.
2. Reread.
3. Circle the words that appear in the note outline below. The words that you circle are called key words. These words convey meaning in a sentence. When you create your outlines, choose key words to help you remember the main ideas of the sentence on which you are taking notes.

Structural Tools and Suggestions
Use Roman numerals (I, II, etc.) for each new paragraph and Arabic numbers (1, 2, 3) for details. Use no more than five details per paragraph, with one to three key words per detail, or note. It's also fun to use symbols for shorthand that you'll remember when you look back on your outlines (↑, #, etc.) later.

Note Outline Model: Economics Defined
    I.   Economics Defined—Goods and Services
        1. production, allocation, use
        2. satisfy, greatest #, people
        3. connected, globally, ↑ important

    II.   Two Major Divisions
        1. macro, micro
        2. macro, systems, interdependence
        3. micro, 1 business, 1 industry

Lesson 2: Some History of Economics

Objective
To learn to take notes while limiting yourself to main ideas.

Source Text

In medieval times the system of feudalism dominated. In this system, the king owned the land, everything on the land, and all of its capacity for production of goods and services. Under the king, various nobles ruled over portions of the land and resources. These nobles decided how to allocate resources among the various people living within their domain. The people were, largely, peasant farmers who worked the land in exchange for protection by the nobles.

During the 16th, 17th, and 18th centuries, mercantilism was the dominant system. This was the system of the merchant, with origins starting earlier as various kingdoms began to increase international (inter-sovereign) trade during medieval times. Mercantilism continues as a system of economics even today. The main tenant of mercantilism is that a given nation should work to increase exports, collecting and hording precious metals in exchange. Manufacturing became more important in this system.

The Industrial Revolution had its roots in the late 18th century, and dramatically expanded throughout the 19th and into the 20th centuries. The Industrial Revolution ushered in an era of machinery and factory systems. The Industrial Revolution was fueled by tremendous advancements in technology through innovation and invention. During this period, the idea of "laissez faire" became popular. This means that economies work best without excessive rules and regulations from the government. This philosophy of economics is a strong factor in capitalism, which favors private ownership.

Karl Marx attacked the capitalistic, "laissez faire" theories of competition and instead favored socialism, marked by greater government control and state ownership over private ownership of assets, companies, and even entire industries.

Assignment
1. Read the source text and study the note outline model for paragraph number one.
2. Circle the words that appear in paragraph number one and in the note outline model. Circle the words or abbreviations in the note outline that do not appear in the text. These words are paraphrased or abbreviated from the text, which means they convey the same meaning in different (and fewer) words. For example, in Lesson 1, the source text, second to last line read, "considering all global issues." We used the word

"interdependence" in our first note outline model to convey the same meaning.

3. Make a key word outline for the second paragraph, using the same idea of limiting each detail to no more than three words.
4. Verbally tell back this portion of the story to your teacher or parent by looking at your key word outline and making the notes into complete sentences. Add in as much detail as you can, but don't worry about remembering all the details. If you need to stop and read the original source text again, that's fine.

Note Outline Model

    I.   Medieval, Feudalism
          1. king, land, productivity
          2. nobles, ruled, portions
          3. nobles, distributed, resources
          4. peasants, work$\leftrightarrow$protection

    II.   Mercantilism, 16th–18th Century

          1. _____

          2. _____

          3. _____

          4. _____

The language of economics requires development of an expanded vocabulary. You should make yourself familiar with some of the jargon (vernacular, tongue, slang, phraseology, or "shop talk") used by economists, politicians, and business executives in communicating ideas relating to matters of economics. Spend some time contemplating the **Key Terms List** found on page 12. If you don't have a working definition for each of these key terms, then take some time to look up the definitions in your dictionary or in an economics text. As you read, write, and learn, feel free to add additional terms that are new to you. Extra space is provided within the Key Terms List for you to make your own additions. For example, you may wish to add the term "Mercantilism" to the list provided.

Key Terms

Advertising	GDP – gross domestic product	Price level	Tax revenue	
Assets		Product differentiation	Trade balance	
Consumption	Imitation	Productivity	Unemployment	
Costs	Imports	Profits	Wages	
Demand	Inflation	Protectionism		
Elasticity	Innovation	Resources		
Employment	Interest rates	Risk		
Energy		Savings		
Exchange	Investment	Social groups		
Exports	Leverage	Substitutes		
FDI - foreign direct investment	Money	Supply		
	Poverty			

Style Tools and Examples

Adverbs ending in "-ly" add to (and strengthen) verbs and give your writing power. Using sentence #1 as an example, choose one, two or three "-ly"s from the list on the next page for the blank spaces in sentences 2 through 4.

1. (Model) The king **eagerly** appointed a new Knight into his feudal system which **mercifully** nurtures **and bravely** protects all peasants of the kingdom.

2. Capitalism has _____ had its affects all over the world, _____ including the former Soviet Union and Eastern European countries.

3. They _____ but _____ provide effective help to the poorest of the poor in a number of countries.

4. The Industrial Revolution has been _____ recognized and _____ acclaimed throughout the world.

Adverbs: "-ly" Words

absolutely	finally	lightly	simply
anxiously	fortunately	masterfully	slowly
blindly	frantically	miraculously	steadily
bravely	frequently	mournfully	stubbornly
calmly	fundamentally	noisily	substantially
carefully	graciously	notably	successfully
certainly	gradually	occasionally	suddenly
cheerfully	heartily	predictably	surely
completely	helpfully	presumably	tactfully
continually	hopefully	primarily	tenderly
conveniently	hopelessly	probably	terribly
critically	humbly	proudly	thoroughly
definitely	immediately	quickly	thoughtfully
diligently	impatiently	quietly	tragically
distinctly	inevitably	reasonably	ultimately
divinely	infinitely	regularly	unhappily
dramatically	instantly	repeatedly	utterly
drastically	joyously	sadly	violently
eagerly	kindly	safely	virtually
easily	knowingly	separately	willingly
energetically	laboriously	seriously	wistfully
evenly	lazily	significantly	
eventually		silently	
faithfully			

"-ly" Collection

Some people like to collect dolls, spoons, cards, bells or even bottle caps. Writers, however, love to collect words. Start right now collecting some "-ly" adverbs from your reading and other subject study. Start building a list on this page, and add to it throughout the year. You will find that a handy list of words is like a "brain expander" letting you skillfully use words you might never have thought of otherwise.

_____   _____   _____

_____   _____   _____

_____   _____   _____

_____   _____   _____

Unit II: Writing From Notes
Lesson 3: Innovation

Objective
To learn how to carefully limit notes and write a summary from them. Key words have already been underlined for you.

Source Text

What precisely constitutes <u>innovation</u> is <u>hard to</u> say and even harder to <u>measure</u>. Innovation is usually thought of as the <u>creation</u> of a <u>better</u> <u>product</u>, service, or process. But, it could also be the <u>substitution</u> of a cheaper <u>material</u> in an existing product, or a better <u>method</u> of marketing, distributing, or supporting a product or service. We often <u>confuse</u> innovation with <u>invention</u>. <u>Inventing</u> is <u>only</u> one <u>part</u> of the creative process.

Innovating takes <u>time</u>, <u>money</u>, and entrepreneurial <u>insight</u>. <u>Two</u> <u>key</u> things <u>characterize</u> the most innovative companies. Innovative companies hire and encourage <u>individuals</u> who are <u>driven</u> by a strong need for personal <u>achievement</u>. Also, they pursue innovation in a <u>systematic</u> manner, constantly <u>searching</u> for ways to <u>change</u> and improve. This leads to a <u>cultural</u> mentality of <u>continuous</u> <u>improvement</u>.

Assignment
1. Read the source text. The outline notes are carefully limited since some sentences contain many details.
2. Following the outline, write two paragraphs about Innovation. Include all of the ideas from the outline in your paragraph, using the "Dress-ups" described on page 17. Underline one of each of the dress-ups from your level. When you write your paragraphs from the outline, write approximately one sentence per note. (For this assignment, there are 5 sentences and, therefore, 5 notes per paragraph, so each of your paragraphs should consist of <u>approximately</u> 5 sentences.)
3. Your first draft should be handwritten, double-spaced, with no erasing.

Cross out any errors and write the corrections in the extra space above. Edit your first draft for spelling, punctuation and grammar as best you can, then have another person (parent, teacher or older sibling) check it as well. When it has been checked and corrected as thoroughly as possible, copy (or type) a final draft. Keep your final draft in this book with each lesson, or in the back separated with a divider.

4. Follow the checksheet on page 18. Your teacher may add (or delete) techniques you know (or don't know) to customize the checklist for your level of challenge. You must have at least one of each dress-up technique for each paragraph. (You may, of course have more than one "-ly" word, etc., but only underline one of each.)

Note Outline Model: Innovation

I. Innovation, hard, to measure

    1. create, better, product

    2. substitute, material, or method

    3. innovation $\oslash$ invention

    4. inventing, only, part

II. Time, money, insight

    1. two, keys, characterize

    2. individuals, driven, achieve

    3. systematic, searching, change

    4. culture, continuous improvement

Style Tools and Examples
"who/which" clauses
From now on, each paragraph you write should contain at least one **adjective clause**, also called a **"who/which" clause**. These allow you to add detail or to connect ideas. Adjective clauses describe nouns and begin with *who, whom, whose,* or *which.* Everyone should complete the practice sentences below, following the first sentence as a model. Use *who* for people and *which* for things. Level B & C students must include a who/which in their composition for this lesson; Level A, in the next lesson.

1. (Model) Managers, <u>who</u> should not be proud, can become surprisingly haughty in a world <u>which</u> rewards innovation.

2. The inventor <u>who</u> _____ could become wealthy <u>which</u> _____ .

3. The Chief Executive, <u>who</u> _____ says that companies <u>which</u> _____ sold for a lot of money.

◦ Invisible "who/which" clauses, Level C
In addition to a "who/which" clause (adjective) clause in every paragraph, Level C students should also put in an invisible "who/which" clause and mark it by underlining the words on either side of where the "which" would be, as shown in the model below. Always put a comma after the noun that precedes the invisible "who/which" clause. For example:

(Visible who)   The king, <u>who</u> was raising his scepter, appeared glorious.
(Invisible who)   The <u>king</u>, <u>raising</u> his scepter, appeared glorious.

Style Note, Levels B & C
Avoid using *is, are, was,* or *were* as the main verb in a "who/which" clause, since they do not give the reader a strong picture of the subject of the sentence, as shown below.

The product, <u>which</u> **was** for a time useful, eventually became obsolete.

Often, by changing the "who/which" clause to an invisible "who/which" clause, you can remove the weak verb without changing the sentence's meaning. For example:

The <u>product</u>, **<u>for</u> a time useful**, eventually became obsolete.

Checksheet for Lesson 3

Levels A, B, & C

Presentation
___ title centered and underlined
___ name, date
___ clearly presented

Mechanics
___ indent paragraphs
___ complete sentences
___ capitals (uppercase)
___ punctuation

Style Tools
___ underline dress-ups (one of each)

Level A

Dress-Ups
"-ly" word ___

Level B

Dress-Ups
"-ly" word ___
"who/which" clause ___

Level C

Dress-Ups
dual "-ly" word ___
"who/which" clause ___
invisible "who/which" clause ___

Lesson 4: The Wealth of Nations

Objective
To practice the skills of taking notes, creating note outlines, and writing summaries from the outlines.

Source Text

Adam Smith was born in Kirkaldy, on the east coast of Scotland in 1723. He studied first at Glasgow University and then at Oxford. In those days, the universities of Scotland were greater centers of learning than those of England, so Smith returned to the north after finishing his studies at Oxford and obtained an academic appointment at Glasgow. It was not, of course, a chair in economics. Economics had not yet been invented as a distinct discipline, even though ancient writings, as early as those of Plato and Aristotle, touched upon concepts of economics. Smith's specialty was moral philosophy.

During his long career, Smith wrote just two books. It was his good fortune, however, to have both bring him immediate fame. His first book was *The Theory of Moral Sentiments*, published in 1759. His second, *The Wealth of Nations*, appeared seventeen years later, in 1776. *The Wealth of Nations* remains today the cornerstone of modern economic theory. The task Smith set for himself was to explain the workings of the economic system—that is, the sources of the "wealth of nations." The greatest source, he discovered, was the division of labor. He found that worker productivity was greatly increased when the tasks involved in making something were finely subdivided allowing each individual to work as a member of a team in social cooperation.

In *The Wealth of Nations*, Smith emphasizes the benefits of economic liberty. He points out that the free, spontaneous interaction of people in the marketplace is the best way to bring about the general benefit of humanity. Finally, he demonstrates that when government attempts to "guide" the market, more harm is done than good.

Assignment
1. Read the source text.
2. In the space below, take notes for the first two paragraphs. You will need to limit your notes, looking for the key words and key ideas very carefully.
3. After you have made your key word outline, verbally tell back the ideas represented by the key words to someone else. If you don't understand why you wrote the words you chose, go back and read the original text again.
4. Using the key words from your note outline, write a 2-paragraph composition entitled, "The Wealth of Nations". Double-space your first draft. Have it edited and then handwrite or type a final draft to keep.

Structural Tools and Suggestions

Whenever you make a note outline, follow the format below.
In the outline, Roman numerals indicate paragraph beginnings (and will later show topic sentences).

Note Outline: The Wealth of Nations

I. Adam Smith, Birth of Economics

1. _____
2. _____
3. _____
4. _____
5. _____
6. _____

II. Wealth of Nations

1. _____
2. _____
3. _____
4. _____
5. _____
6. _____
7. _____
8. _____

Style Tools and Examples
"because" clauses

Like the "who/which" clause, a "because" clause can be used to give more detail or to connect ideas. There is no special technique involved in using the word "because" in your paragraph, but you should be careful not to create a fragment. If you start your sentence with the word "because", then you will need to have a comma in that sentence. (Some teachers do not like sentences that start with "because", and if that's your situation, then you must not do it; try the word "since" or "as".)

1. (Model) Adam Smith claimed increased productivity through division of labor **because everyone shares a common motivation.**

2. (Model) **Because Adam Smith had a deep understanding of moral philosophy**, everything he said about economics reflected this moral understanding.

3. Smith returned to Scotland because _____

    _____

    _____.

4. Smith emphasized the benefits of economic liberty because _____

    _____

    _____.

5. Because of the spontaneous interaction of people in the marketplace,

    _____

    _____.

Note the fragments, or incomplete sentences. Also, note the necessary commas in the correct example below.

1. Because some businessmen were well educated. (Incorrect)

2. Because some businessmen were well educated, they worked best as members of a team, focused on continuous improvement. (Correct)

Just for Fun

Look up "invisible hand" on the Internet or at your local public library. See how Adam Smith's work continues to generate controversy on the subject of economic theory. If you like, you may use your research to enrich your writing for this assignment. Even though the term "invisible hand" does not appear in your source text for this assignment you will understand immediately how the concepts connect, and you might like to use this key term to condense a concept that would otherwise take several sentences to explain.

Checksheet for Lesson 4

	Paragraphs	I.	II.
Levels A, B, & C	**Level A**		
Presentation	**Dress-Ups**		
___ title centered and underlined	"-ly" word	___	___
___ name, date	"who/which" clause	___	___
___ clearly presented			
Mechanics	**Level B**		
___ indent paragraphs	**Dress-Ups**		
___ complete sentences	"-ly" word	___	___
___ capitals (uppercase)	"who/which" clause	___	___
___ punctuation	"because" clause	___	___
Style Tools	**Level C**		
___ underline dress-ups (one of each)	**Dress-Ups**		
	dual "-ly" word	___	___
	"who/which" clause	___	___
	invisible "who/which" clause	___	___
	(no "to be" verbs with		
	"who/which")		
	"because" clause	___	___

Lesson 5: Opportunity Cost

Objective
To further practice the skills of taking notes, creating note outlines, and writing summaries from them.

Source Text

Cost is a concept central to the economic way of thinking. In a world of scarcity, it is rare to get something for nothing. Typically, we must bear costs to obtain benefits. The key cost concept in economics is that of opportunity cost—the cost of doing something, as measured in terms of the value of the lost opportunity to pursue the best alternative activity with the same time or resources.

In many cases, the opportunity cost of doing something is properly measured in terms of money out-of-pocket. For example, the opportunity cost of spending a dollar for a nutritious glass of milk is the loss of the opportunity to spend the same dollar on a not-so-nutritious candy bar. In other cases, activities that have no or limited money cost have important opportunity costs in terms of time. For example, an hour spent nurturing your brain by studying is an hour not available for wasting your brain away by watching television.

Considering opportunity cost should automatically lead us to consider value as well. Of course, what we value in life is dependent upon the virtues we practice. If we value the wrong things, then our calculations of opportunity cost lose their meaning. For example, do you value freedom, or the opportunity to have the government send you a check each month? Do you value wholesome, hard work or the opportunity to relax? Do you value entrepreneurial enthusiasm or the perceived security of a job in a major corporation? How about university?

If you are already committed to attending a college or university, then you should do a financial plan for each year considering things like tuition, fees, books, supplies, laptop, transportation, housing, food and other essentials. Your out-of-pocket budget allows you to make sure you have enough in savings, scholarships, loans, and parents' contributions to make ends meet. But suppose you are making the more basic decision of whether to continue your education or pursue some alternative career pattern that does not require further education. Then it is the opportunity cost of college/university that you should take into account, weighing this cost against the benefit of possibly greater future earnings (unless you decide to do something entrepreneurial) or greater personal satisfaction that you expect to get from higher education.

Assignment
1. Read the source text.
2. Take notes. Consider key words from only the third and fourth paragraphs of source text for the purposes of note taking in this lesson. You will be challenged to limit your key words for the very long sentences of the final paragraph of source text. You can do it!
3. Write a two-paragraph composition about opportunity cost.

Note Outline: Opportunity Cost

I. Considering Value

1. _____
2. _____
3. _____
4. _____
5. _____
6. _____
7. _____

II. How about College/University?

1. _____
2. _____
3. _____
4. _____

Style Tools and Examples
Quality Adjectives (Level B now, Level A later).
An adjective describes (or tells more about) a noun (person, place, thing or idea). For example, any word you write in the sentence below is probably an adjective. Try it with any of these words: mysterious, bright, blue, dangerous, thick, etc.

The _____ pen rolled off the _____ table.

The Dutch merchant raised the _____ tulip to demonstrate his wealth and success in the eyes of the world.

The young man purchased a _____ candy bar instead of buying that sensible glass of milk.

Dual Adjectives, Level C

From now on, write at least one set of dual adjectives in every paragraph (and underline one set.) Dual adjectives modify the same noun, as in the example below.

Wearily Adam wrote the **massive, engaging** book.

Massive and *engaging* are dual adjectives describing *book*. Make sure that the two adjectives you use are not synonyms, as in: "Adam had faith in his **precious, dear** theory."

Banned Adjectives

Some adjectives are "weak" or "cheap" in that they do not create a strong image or feeling for the reader. The words big, small, bad, good, and cool can easily be replaced by more descriptive choices. Refer to the Banned Adjectives list below to find alternatives to use in your compositions.

Add your own synonyms in the spaces provided. Use a thesaurus or keep a list of words found in your reading.

big	small	bad	good	cool / fun
sizable	tiny	lousy	superb	interesting
gigantic	miniscule	wicked	fantastic	captivating
huge	petite	unpleasant	admirable	fascinating
enormous	slight	horrible	excellent	challenging
immense	puny	terrible	wholesome	exciting
massive	trivial	evil	stupendous	stylish
grand	minor	awful	wonderful	
_____	_____	_____	_____	_____
_____	_____	_____	_____	_____
_____	_____	_____	_____	_____
_____	_____	_____	_____	_____
_____	_____	_____	_____	_____
_____	_____	_____	_____	_____
_____	_____	_____	_____	_____

Checksheet for Lesson 5

	Paragraphs	I.	II.
Levels A, B, & C	**Level A**		
Presentation	**Dress-Ups**		
___ title centered and underlined	"-ly" word	___	___
___ name, date	"who/which" clause	___	___
___ clearly presented	"because" clause	___	___
Mechanics	**Level B**		
___ indent paragraphs			
___ complete sentences	**Dress-Ups**		
___ capitals (uppercase)	"-ly" word	___	___
___ punctuation	"who/which" clause	___	___
	"because" clause	___	___
	quality adjective	___	___
Style Tools			
___ underline dress-ups (one of each)	**Level C**		
___ no "banned" adjectives			
	Dress-Ups		
	dual "-ly" word	___	___
	"who/which" clause	___	___
	invisible "who/which" clause	___	___
	(no "to be" verbs with "who/which")		
	"because" clause	___	___
	dual adjectives	___	___

Unit III: Summarizing Narrative Stories
Lesson 6: We'll Stash Your Trash in a Flash

Objective
To learn how to summarize narrative stories, a step toward reviewing and critiquing books and movies. In Unit III, you will create outlines following the Narrative Story Model. This system of creating outlines will be useful when you summarize long or short stories, books or movies, plays, videos or speeches. In each case you will follow a 3-paragraph Narrative Story Model.

Source Text

Brian Scudamore started his company 1-800-GOT-JUNK? in 1989 straight out of high school with $700 and a beat-up old pick-up truck. Today they have over 300 franchise partners across North America with a true national presence—they are in 47 of North America's top 50 cities. Scudamore was a risk-taker, but firm in his vision. "With a vision of creating the 'FedEx' of junk removal," says Scudamore, "I dropped out of University with just one year left to become a fulltime JUNKMAN! Yes, my father, a liver transplant surgeon, was not impressed to say the least."

Many entrepreneurs minimize their risks by outsourcing to contractors. Scudamore chose a different route. "I hired my first employee a week after I started. I knew I needed the help. His name was David Sniderman—a good friend of mine. I really didn't know yet how to hire so I just asked a buddy." It may have started as a matter of simply not knowing what else to do, but it became a philosophical issue for him. "I always believed in hiring people. I felt that if I wasn't willing to make the investment then I was questioning my own faith in the business." On the other hand, he's a big believer in letting other people share some of the risk. His choice of franchising as a business model allowed him rapid growth without having to turn to outside investors or other funding sources. "It's the ultimate leverage model. People pay you a fee up-front to help them grow. Rather than lose control of my vision by going public—I chose franchising." Brian has managed to retain 100% ownership and bootstrapped the business solely out of cash flow—something that is very rare these days.

Although this is a simple business, they couldn't possibly have grown this quickly without technology. Taking a low tech business and putting a high tech spin on it allowed them to rapidly distinguish themselves from their competition. All calls come into a central 1-800-GOT-JUNK? call center where they do all the booking and dispatch for their franchise partners. Franchise partners then assess all of their real time reports, schedules, customer info, etc., off of JUNKNET, their corporate intranet. This allows franchise partners to get into business quickly, and to focus solely on growth.

1-800-GOT-JUNK? did over $35 Million in sales during their fiscal year 2005—not a bad return on a $700.00 investment! The company continues to grow year-after-year, building themselves into the world's largest junk removal service—now going international.

Article reprinted with permission.

Assignment
1. Read the source text.
2. The first paragraph of a 3-paragraph composition appears on page 30. Using the Narrative Story Model Note Outline as a guide, write the other two paragraphs, following the checklist on page 32.
3. Save your work, as we will revisit this narrative model and critique process in Unit IX.

Structural Tools and Suggestions
This outline format is different from the one you learned in Units I and II. Rather than taking key words from the source text, use the story sequence chart to ask yourself questions about the story. Put the answers in a three-paragraph outline format. The information you put in your outline may not be in the same order as it appears on the original story. Paragraphs should be of approximately equal length. In the last sentence of your last paragraph, include 2–3 key words that also appear in your composition's title. You may wish to wait until writing the last paragraph to decide the title. Your title should repeat the key words of the last sentence.

Narrative Story Model Note Outline
We'll Stash Your Trash in a Flash

I. Brian Scudamore, entrepreneur
    1. started 1989, $700, old truck
    2. university dropout, fulltime junkman
    3. hired friend, David Sniderman
    4. believe hiring, believe in business
	<u>I. Characters and Setting</u>
	Who is in the story?
	What are they like?
	Where did they live?
	What was their situation?
	When did they live?

II. How to Grow the Business?
    1. franchising, up-front fees
    2. share risks, others grow
    3. rapid growth, no outside investors
    4. fund from cash flow
	<u>II. Conflict</u>
	What was the problem?
	What happened?
	What did they think?
	What did they say?
	What did they do?

III. Competitive Differentiation
    1. utilize technology, JUNKNET
    2. call center, booking, dispatch
    3. maintain control, support partners
    4. start quick, focus growth
    5. $35 Million, 300 partners, 47/50 cities
	<u>III. Climax</u>
	How was the problem solved?
	How could the problem be solved?
	What is the moral message?

Title repeats key words of last sentence

Model First Paragraph: We'll Stash Your Trash in a Flash

1-800-GOT-JUNK? started with <u>absolutely</u> nothing but one <u>hopelessly</u> <u>ancient</u> pick-up truck and $700 in cash. The founder, Brian Scudamore, <u>enthusiastically</u> completed high school in 1989 <u>because</u> he wanted to launch his business even before attending university. The business grew <u>tremendously</u> <u>which</u> inspired Brian to become a fulltime junkman without a university diploma. David Sniderman, <u>who</u> was Brian's best friend, became the first person Brian hired. <u>Because</u> he wished to <u>bravely</u> demonstrate his <u>immense, unwavering</u> faith in the business, Brian continued to hire employees <u>as</u> the business grew.	who? characters? where? - place when? - time

Style Tools and Examples (Levels B & C now, Level A later)

The next dress-up element is an adverbial clause, which begins with one of the clausal starters shown here. In each paragraph you write from now on, include and underline an adverb clause that begins with one of these clausal starters. "Because" can also be an adverbial starter, although you will use the *because* along with another clause for several more lessons. Note that the first letter of the words: *when, while, where, as, since, if, although,* when said in that order, can create the Web site-looking acronym "www.asia"

ADVERBIAL CLAUSAL STARTERS:
when while where as since if although (because)

Brian questioned his franchise partners...

<u>when</u> they gathered together.
<u>while</u> coffee was being served.
<u>where</u> they would feel most comfortable.
<u>as</u> soon as he arrived at the office.
<u>since</u> they had the information he needed.
as <u>if</u> he expected customer service reports.
<u>although</u> he was exhausted from hard work.
<u>because</u> the customer must always be satisfied.

Practice creating adverbial clauses with the following examples. Ask your parent or teacher for suggestions if you can't think of anything. If you can't write small enough to fit your clause on one line, use a blank sheet of paper instead. (This applies to any of the fill-in-the-blank exercises in this book.)

Brian Scudamore succeeded in business...

when _____ .

while _____ .

where _____ .

as _____ .

since _____ .

if _____ .

although _____ .

Brian believes that everyone can excel...

when _____ .

while _____ .

where _____ .

as _____ .

since _____ .

if _____ .

although _____ .

Checksheet for Lesson 6

	Paragraphs	II.	III.

Levels A, B, & C

Presentation
___ title centered and underlined
___ name, date
___ clearly presented

Mechanics
___ indent paragraphs
___ complete sentences
___ capitals (uppercase)
___ punctuation

Structure
___ follows model
___ paragraphs roughly equal size
___ title reflects key words of last
    sentence

Style Tools
___ underline dress-ups (one of each)
___ no "banned" adjectives

Level A

  Dress-Ups
  "-ly" word   ____ ____
  "who/which" clause   ____ ____
  "because" clause   ____ ____
  quality adjective   ____ ____

Level B

  Dress-Ups
  "-ly" word   ____ ____
  "who/which" clause   ____ ____
  (no "to be" verbs with
  "who/which")   ____ ____
  "because" clause   ____ ____
  quality adjective   ____ ____
  adverbial clause (www.asia)   ____ ____

Level C

  Dress-Ups
  dual "-ly" word   ____ ____
  "who/which" clause
  invisible "who/which" clause   ____ ____
  (no "to be" verbs with
  "who/which")   ____ ____
  "because" clause   ____ ____
  dual adjectives   ____ ____
  adverbial clause (www.asia)   ____ ____

Lesson 7: The FruitGuys

Objective
To practice summarizing narrative stories while thinking about entrepreneurial success.

Source Text

Chris Mittelstaedt started The FruitGuys in 1998 immediately after learning that his wife was pregnant. Chris had been earning $9.50/hr in a temporary job, and he felt there was no time to waste. He wanted to launch his dream before the baby arrived. Today, The FruitGuys serve farm-fresh produce to over 3,000 corporate customers nation-wide. They are a multimillion-dollar enterprise employing more than 40 people. According to Inc.com, The FruitGuys were one of the fastest-growing businesses in the US for 2008 and 2009.

The FruitGuys isn't the only thing that continues to grow—Chris' family has grown, too. Chris and his wife now have three children and enjoy their family home in San Francisco very much. His family is Chris' most critical and trusted body of fruit tasters!

Getting to where he is today wasn't always easy. Chris started with a regional approach serving the San Francisco Bay Area with its load of high-tech and dot.com companies. In 2000, while The FruitGuys were still a fledgling operation, the tech-bubble bust brought down many of Chris' clients. This crisis almost drove Chris out of business. At the time, he found himself stuck with a lot of uncollectable accounts, but he persevered. After the tech-bubble, Chris recovered by restructuring his business to include a strict credit policy. He reduced his fixed costs and increased his variable costs. He also expanded the business nationally to secure a diversified customer base.

Today, Chris enjoys dressing up as a banana while passing out fruit to people on the street. He also spends time writing about the farmers and fruit so central to his dream of promoting improved health in the modern workplace. Chris remains true to his original vision of developing a unique and viable business while advancing the wellbeing of people. Chris and The FruitGuys have created a practical and proven method to address the rising costs of workplace healthcare and overall corporate productivity. Learn more at www.fruitguys.com

Written with permission.

Assignment
1. Read the source text.
2. Construct a 3-paragraph outline which follows the Narrative Story Model, by asking questions about the story.
3. From your outline, write a double-spaced, 3-paragraph composition.

4. Proofread your composition, making sure you included all the elements of presentation, structure, mechanics, and style. Get a second opinion if possible. When you are satisfied, prepare a final draft.

Structural Tools and Suggestions

You may limit details in each paragraph, including only 3 or 4 details in one, perhaps 5 in another.

When written out, paragraphs should be approximately the same size to keep your composition balanced, and each paragraph should be at least four sentences long.

If the story is short on details, imagine what the characters might have been thinking, feeling, or saying, and add in some content that complements the story. For example, in this story, you might imagine that the entire Mittelstaedt family enjoys dressing up in fruit costumes to help promote the business. Include some dialog between the grapes and the banana (Chris.)

Narrative Story Model Outline: The FruitGuys

I.

1. _____
2. _____
3. _____
4. _____
5. _____

♦ Who is in the story?
♦ What were they like?
♦ Where did they go?
♦ When did the action occur?

II.

1. _____
2. _____
3. _____
4. _____
5. _____

♦ What was the problem?
♦ What happened?
♦ What did they think?
♦ What did they say?
♦ What did they do?

III.

1. _____
2. _____
3. _____
4. _____
5. _____

♦ Climax
♦ How was the problem solved?
♦ What is the moral message?
♦ Title repeats key words from last sentence.

Style Tools and Example (Levels B & C now, Level A later)
Strong Verbs
Strengthen your writing by using powerful verbs rather than "weak" ones. Examine the sentences below as they progress from weak and ordinary to powerful.

1. (ordinary verb) He **knocked** on the door.
2. (more powerful verb) He **pounded** on the door.
3. (with an adverb added) He **vigorously pounded** on the door.
4. (dual power verbs) He **vigorously pounded and kicked** the door.
5. (dual "-ly"s and dual verbs) He **loudly and violently pounded on and kicked** at the door.

Dual Verbs, Level C
From now on, write dual verbs into each paragraph to strengthen your compositions. Note the conjunctions – *and, even, then,* and *but.*

He was invited to **and** joined in the franchise agreement.
Brian whistled **even** danced during his work day.
Chris inspected **then** purchased the fruit.
She sang **but** faltered half way through.

Triple Verbs, Advanced (optional)
For advanced students, include at least one set of triple verbs in each paragraph of your compositions.

The workers **hoisted, tipped, and poured** the junk out.
Kites **glided, dipped, and soared** in the midday sky.

Banned Verbs

Add your own synonyms in the spaces provided.

go/went	see/saw	say/said	eat/ate	think/thought
travel/ed	notice/d	yell/ed	gobble/d	ponder/ed
journey/ed	eye/d	whisper/ed	devour/ed	believe/d
wander/ed	peer/ed	command/ed	munch/ed	imagine/d
run/ran	glimpse/d	ask/ed	slurp/ed	remember/ed
adventured	observed	whined	chomped	marveled
hiked	wathed	shooted	consumed	brain stormed
			inhaled	

36

Checksheet for Lesson 7

	Paragraphs		I.	II.	III.

Levels A, B, & C

Presentation
___ title centered and underlined
___ name, date
___ clearly presented

Mechanics
___ indent paragraphs
___ complete sentences
___ capitals (uppercase)
___ punctuation

Structure
___ follows model
___ paragraphs roughly equal size
___ title reflects key words of last
       sentence

Style Tools
___ underline dress-ups (one of each)
___ no "banned" adjectives
___ no "banned" verbs (B & C only)

Level A

Dress-Ups
"-ly" word ___ ___ ___
"who/which" clause ___ ___ ___
"because" clause ___ ___ ___
 quality adjective ___ ___ ___

Level B

Dress-Ups
"-ly" word ___ ___ ___
"who/which" clause ___ ___ ___
(no "to be" verbs with
"who/which")
"because" clause ___ ___ ___
 quality adjective ___ ___ ___
 adverbial clause
(www.asia) ___ ___ ___
 strong verb ___ ___ ___

Level C

Dress-Ups
dual "-ly" word ___ ___ ___
"who/which" clause ___ ___ ___
invisible "who/which"
clause
(no "to be" verbs with
"who/which") ___ ___ ___
"because" clause ___ ___ ___
dual adjectives ___ ___ ___
adverbial clause
(www.asia)
dual (or triple) verbs ___ ___ ___

Lesson 8: Making a Business out of Air

Objective
To practice summarizing. In this lesson, limiting becomes important because you will summarize a much longer story.

Source Text

Air Products and Chemicals, Inc. (Air Products), is an American success story and one of the world's major suppliers of industrial gases. The story of Air Products is exciting—full of struggle, determination, crisis, and heroic endeavor. Air Products grew out of the vision and drive of one individual, Leonard Pool. In 1940, Leonard Pool took a daring chance by making a revolutionary and innovative idea of his into a reality. Today, seventy years later, the impact of this venture can be seen in many aspects of our everyday lives. With the start of Air Products, Leonard Pool created the first ever on-site oxygen plants. Since then the company has grown into a $10 billion dollar enterprise, employing over 20,000 people worldwide and has developed plants in over thirty countries around the globe.

The industrial gas business is a very interesting one. The main resource and the starting material for this industry is air. That's right. The very air you are breathing right now. The air you breathe is made up mostly of nitrogen gas (about 79%). The next ingredient is oxygen gas (about 20%). The remaining 1% is made up of noble gases like argon plus various contaminants like carbon monoxide, nitrous oxide, and others. Air is liquefied at a special facility called an air separation plant. At this plant, the liquefied air is distilled and purified—just like you might distill alcohol, but at much lower boiling points—into pure liquid nitrogen, liquid oxygen, and liquid argon. These cryogenic (super cold) liquids are transported in specialty tanker trucks across the highways. Perhaps, you have seen a big truck with a tank labeled "cryogenic liquid—liquid nitrogen, or liquid oxygen, or liquid argon?"

What are the uses of liquid nitrogen? Well, all McDonald's hamburger patties are frozen with liquid nitrogen. The quick-freeze process helps to maintain the cell structure of the meat and protect it for extended transportation. Liquid nitrogen boils (transforms from liquid to gas) at -320 degrees Fahrenheit. That's pretty darn cold! Many foods are flash-frozen using liquid nitrogen.

Liquid oxygen is stored in a special tank outside every major hospital in the world. The liquid is converted back into pure oxygen gas and transported through an extensive piping system everywhere in the hospital. If you've ever been in a hospital bed and received a mask with pure oxygen to help you breathe easier, chances are that the nurse plugged your line into the hospital's central piping system to supply your breathing mask.

Liquid argon is also stored and then converted back into pure gas to be used as a specialty inert atmosphere for a variety of industrial processes. For example, the microprocessor in your computer was built upon a chip of silicon. That silicon had to be grown from a single crystal in a specialized furnace. This production process is highly sensitive to gaseous impurities. The molten silicon will react with nitrogen or oxygen in the air to form silicon nitride or silicon dioxide and ruin the foundation of your computer's chip even before it has a chance to become a microprocessor. So, the inert, purified, argon gas atmosphere protects the silicon during this initial formation process.

There are many more industrial gases and many more uses for them, here we have just named three.

By making a customer's plant on-site, Leonard Pool was able to eliminate the costly transportation of oxygen from a large, centralized air separation plant to the customer's factory or use point. Large users of oxygen, like steel mills for example, could have their own source of pure oxygen produced on-site and supplied directly to their points of use without waiting for truck delivery, and at a fraction of the cost. This on-site approach allowed Leonard to enter an already established market with significant competitors and to carve out a niche for his new company. From this starting point, Leonard was able to establish and grow Air Products into a market leader.

World War II provided a significant opportunity for Leonard's plan as steel mills were ramping up production to meet the growing demands of the war effort. Also, Leonard found a way to design and deliver smaller, mobile generators which could be used on military bases to supply oxygen for the crews of high-flying aircraft. High pressure gas cylinders inside aircraft would explode when hit by enemy gunfire. The Army Air Forces decided to store the oxygen aboard aircraft in a liquid state. They also wanted generators of liquid oxygen which had to be operational on aircraft repair ships serving in the Pacific. Since the pitch and yaw of a ship disturbed the flow of gas and liquid in the distillation column, a difficult engineering problem had to be solved. Finally, Air Products had to train non-technical people in the operation and maintenance of these mobile air separation generators.

Words like entrepreneurship, sales, finance, engineering, and technology are central to the history of Air Products. The enduring style of Air Products—its customer-focus and its emphasis on sales and growth—emerged from the interactions of Leonard Pool's personality, the engineering skills of his colleagues, and the opportunities offered by the industrial gas business. Multinational, technology-based firms like Air Products are an important part of American society and of the global economy.

Assignment

1. Read the source text.
2. Create a 3-paragraph outline, carefully following the Narrative Story Model given in Lesson 6. Handwrite your outline into the space provided below.
3. Following your outline & checksheet, write a 3-paragraph, double-spaced summary from your outline. Edit, get help, and when you are satisfied, rewrite or type your composition.

Structural Tools and Suggestions

Don't forget to balance your composition by maintaining approximately the same size for each paragraph. In the conclusion, you are welcome to comment on what the moral, message or lesson of this story might be. Remember to use dramatic words from your last sentence to create a title that grabs the reader's attention.

Narrative Story Model Outline: Making a Business out of Air

I. _____	◆Who is in the story? ◆What were they like? ◆Where did they go? ◆When did the action occur?
1. _____	
2. _____	
3. _____	
4. _____	
5. _____	
II. _____	◆What was the problem? ◆What happened? ◆What did they think? ◆What did they say? ◆What did they do?
1. _____	
2. _____	
3. _____	
4. _____	
5. _____	

III. _____

    1. _____

    2. _____

    3. _____

    4. _____

    5. _____

♦Climax
♦How was the problem solved?
♦What is the moral message?
♦Title repeats key words from last sentence.

Possible Adjectives

_____	_____	_____	_____
_____	_____	_____	_____
_____	_____	_____	_____
_____	_____	_____	_____
_____	_____	_____	_____
_____	_____	_____	_____
_____	_____	_____	_____
_____	_____	_____	_____

Checksheet for Lesson 8

	Paragraphs	I.	II.	III.

Levels A, B, & C

Presentation
___ title centered and underlined
___ name, date
___ clearly presented

Mechanics
___ indent paragraphs
___ complete sentences
___ capitals (uppercase)
___ punctuation

Structure
___ follows model
___ paragraphs roughly equal size
___ title reflects key words of last
sentence

Style Tools
___ underline dress-ups (one of each)
___ no "banned" adjectives
___ no "banned" verbs (B & C only)

Level A

Dress-Ups
"-ly" word ___ ___ ___
"who/which" clause ___ ___ ___
"because" clause ___ ___ ___
quality adjective ___ ___ ___

Level B

Dress-Ups
"-ly" word ___ ___ ___
"who/which" clause ___ ___ ___
(no "to be" verbs with
"who/which")
"because" clause ___ ___ ___
quality adjective ___ ___ ___
adverbial clause
(www.asia) ___ ___ ___
strong verb ___ ___ ___

Level C

Dress-Ups
dual "-ly" word ___ ___ ___
"who/which" clause ___ ___ ___
invisible "who/which"
clause
(no "to be" verbs with
"who/which") ___ ___ ___
"because" clause ___ ___ ___
dual adjectives ___ ___ ___
adverbial clause
(www.asia) ___ ___ ___
dual (or triple) verbs ___ ___ ___

Lesson 9: What's in a Tulip?

Objective

To learn to rewrite narrative stories, using a given plot or presentation structure but changing the characters and setting.

Source Text

An economic bubble happens when a financial market booms, expands beyond reasonable measures without checks and balances, and then erupts and collapses like a bursting balloon. The first economic bubble and subsequent collapse happened during the 1620s and 1630s. Expanding trade enabled Dutch merchants to build substantial wealth and surplus income. The Dutch fell in love with rare varieties of tulips and came to cherish them as symbols of wealth. According to financial historian Edward Chancellor, "In 1624, a Semper Augustus fetched the handsome sum of 1,200 florins, an amount sufficient to purchase a small Amsterdam town house at the time." The Semper Augustus is a variety of tulip. Because tulips could only be grown at certain times of the year, the market developed contracts for future delivery, secured by borrowed money. This practice of leveraging (buying stuff with lots of borrowed money) drove up prices to incredible levels. Some reports claim that the best bulbs reached a price as high as 4,000 florins by 1637.

One Viceroy tulip bulb was supposedly worth the equivalent of "twenty-seven tons of wheat, fifty tons of rye, four fat oxen, eight fat pigs, twelve fat sheep, two hogsheads of wine, four turns of beer, two tons of butter, three tons of cheese, a bed with linen, a wardrobe of clothes and a silver beaker," according to Edward Chancellor. As prices climbed, word spread, attracting more and more local investors as well as foreign investors into the market—further inflating prices. For a short time it seemed that fortunes came to those who bought and sold tulip contracts. Modest tradesmen got into the game by taking out loans against their own homes and other assets.

The collapse came on February 3, 1637. Nobody knows why that particular day was the dark day of collapse—it just was. Prices fell so catastrophically that a government commission had to untangle the mess created by the tulip contracts. That government commission made a declaration stating that each futures contract could be annulled by paying just 3.5 percent of the originally agreed upon price. Although the Dutch economy did not collapse, a great many people suffered loss.

Today, the Dutch still love tulips. However, their love affair is tempered with realistic expectations, practical and prudent application, and the removal of ego, image and false perception from the equation.

Assignment
1. Read the source text.
2. Create a 3-paragraph outline following the Narrative Story Model. Keep to a maximum of five details per paragraph. Limiting is vital.
3. Using your outline, write a double-spaced, 3-paragraph composition, describing the Dutch tulip bubble of the 17th century. Use your checksheet to make sure you include all the required elements, have it edited, then rewrite or type a final version.
4. Change things around. For example, instead of happening in Holland, your story could take place in current day America. We have had plenty of our own bubbles in the last ninety years. Or, perhaps you would like to imagine a future bubble—one still in the making. This technique of changing characters and setting but keeping the basic report can be used for creative writing practice with almost any story.

Narrative Story Outline: What's in a Tulip?

I. _____

    1. _____

    2. _____

    3. _____

    4. _____

    5. _____

II. _____

    1. _____

    2. _____

    3. _____

    4. _____

    5. _____

III. _____

    1. _____

    2. _____

    3. _____

    4. _____

    5. _____

Style Tools and Examples (Levels B & C)
Sentence Openers, Part 1

Using the six sentence openers taught in this book, you can improve the flow of your writing and add variety to your paragraphs. As you learn each opener, include it in every paragraph you write and indicate it by placing its number (found below) in the margin. Here are the first three:

❶ **Subject openers** begin with nouns, pronouns or the articles *a, an,* and *the*. (Subject openers are the most common openers, so they should be very easy to use.)

noun:	**Sagas** are stories about real people's challenges.
pronoun:	**He** never forgot his boss, who had successfully invested.
The:	**The** son begged his father for help.
A/an:	**A** sumptuous feast awaited him at the Imperial Hotel.

❷ **Prepositional openers:** Any preposition can be used in a prepositional opener:

Near the ocean	**With** her mother	**After** the storm	**Among** friends
Inside the palace	**In** the beginning	**On** the third day	**At** once

❸ **"-ly" or adverb openers:** When using an "-ly" word as a dress-up, it comes in the middle of sentences. Here "-ly" words are openers:

> **Angrily** the manager dismissed her employee.
> **Lovingly** the native people welcomed them.

Note: This "-ly" opener does not count as the "-ly" dress-up; from now on you'll have at least two "-ly" words in each paragraph: one in the middle (or at the end) of a sentence and one as the first word in a sentence.

Practice: Rewrite the #1 sentence below as a #2 (prepositional) opener, and as a #3 (ly) opener:

❶ The businessman was angry about his lost investment.

❷ *Inside their office,* _____.

❸ *Angrily,* _____.

Prepositions

about	aside from	beyond	inside	opposite	toward
above	at	by	instead	out	under
according to	away from	concerning	into	outside	underneath
across	because of	despite	like	over	unlike
after	before	down	minus	past	until
against	behind	during	near	regarding	up
along	below	except	of	since	upon
amid	beneath	for	off	through	with
among	beside	from	on	throughout	within
around	between	in	onto	to	without

More Practice: Rewrite the #1 sentence below as a #2 (prepositional) opener, and as a #3 (ly) opener:

❶ The young man finally found a job with a multinational corporation.

❷ _____.

❸ _____.

❶ The manager was happy to assist many young people.

❷ _____.

❸ _____.

❶ Asia consistently leads the way in attracting foreign investment.

❷ _____.

❸ _____.

❶ The young lady was completely exhausted from working so hard.

❷ _____ .

❸ _____ .

Checksheet for Lesson 9

| | Paragraphs | I. | II. | III. |

Levels A, B, & C

Presentation
___ title centered and underlined
___ name, date
___ clearly presented

Mechanics
___ indent paragraphs
___ complete sentences
___ capitals (uppercase)
___ punctuation

Structure
___ follows model
___ paragraphs roughly equal size
___ title reflects key words of last sentence

Style Tools
___ underline dress-ups (one of each)
___ no "banned" adjectives
___ no "banned" verbs
___ put sentence opener numbers in the margins (B & C only)

Sentence Openers (B & C only)
(Use all three in each paragraph.)
___ ❶ subject
___ ❷ preposition
___ ❸ "-ly" word

Paragraphs   I.   II.   III.

Level A

Dress-Ups
"-ly" word   ___ ___ ___
"who/which" clause   ___ ___ ___
"because" clause   ___ ___ ___
quality adjective   ___ ___ ___
adverbial clause
(www.asia)   ___ ___ ___

Level B

Dress-Ups
"-ly" word   ___ ___ ___
"who/which" clause
(no "to be" verbs with
"who/which")   ___ ___ ___
"because" clause   ___ ___ ___
quality adjective   ___ ___ ___
adverbial clause
(www.asia)   ___ ___ ___
strong verb   ___ ___ ___
sentence openers   ___ ___ ___

Level C

Dress-Ups
dual "-ly" word   ___ ___ ___
"who/which" clause   ___ ___ ___
invisible "who/which"
clause
(no "to be" verbs with
"who/which")   ___ ___ ___
"because" clause   ___ ___ ___
dual adjectives   ___ ___ ___
adverbial clause
(www.asia)   ___ ___ ___
dual (or triple) verbs   ___ ___ ___
sentence openers   ___ ___ ___

50

Unit IV: Summarizing References
Lesson 10: The Economics of Alternative Energy

Objective
To learn to take notes and create an outline for reference from academic material. As always, the main goal is to rewrite the materials in your own words using only your notes. Note taking from references does not follow the model used in Unit III. Instead, it is like the system described in Units II and I with even greater limiting. Also, you will learn to organize facts into paragraphs using the topic/clincher model. The following source material is lengthy and somewhat complex. Take your time with it and get help from your teacher if you don't understand some part or parts.

Source Text

For the foreseeable future, the major energy alternatives to oil and gas are coal, nuclear power, and solar power. Strictly speaking, coal and conventional nuclear power are nonrenewable energy sources like oil and natural gas, but they present rather different economic problems in that the availability of known fuel reserves is not the main barrier to their wider use. Solar power is genuinely renewable.

Like oil and natural gas, coal is a fossil fuel; but unlike them, its use as an energy source is limited on the demand rather than the supply side. U.S. coal reserves are enormous—enough to last at least five hundred years. What is more, mining capacity already in place is not even being used fully. The major factor constraining the greater use of coal as an energy source is the cost of burning it in an environmentally acceptable way. This raises two sets of economic issues—those concerned with setting the environmental standards for use of coal and those concerned with meeting the standards.

The major pollutant in coal is sulphur, which when burned, produces sulphur dioxide. In urban areas, air pollution from unrestricted burning of coal is a major public health hazard. In agricultural and forest areas, sulphur dioxide pollution causes acid rain, which damages vegetation. And in wilderness areas, such as those of the coal-rich Western states, burning coal is a threat to visibility and hence to the attractiveness of national parks and other outdoor recreation areas.

Work is underway on a number of technologies for the clean burning of coal. Presently, most coal is burned directly to fire boilers generating electricity, with the pollutants scrubbed out of the stack gases before they are released into the air. The major alternative focus is on preliminary conversion of coal into a clean synthetic fuel that can be burned without elaborate pollution control devices at the point of use. One technique, known as solvent refining, produces a liquid substitute for oil. Another technique bakes the coal and blasts it with air to produce a clean, flammable mixture of carbon monoxide and hydrogen, know as producer gas. This gas was widely manufactured in local gasworks during the early 1900s, but it was displaced by natural gas when long-distance pipelines were built. Although producer gas is unlikely to be reintroduced in the residential market, many industrial users are now finding it profitable to build on-site producer gas plants to meet their own needs.

Because nuclear energy is used almost exclusively to produce electricity, its major competitor is coal. It is appropriate, then, to cast the discussion of the economics of nuclear power in the form of a comparison with coal. The basic economics of nuclear power versus coal is simple to state: nuclear power plants are more expensive to build but cheaper to operate. Once built, the coal plant would gulp a hundred-car trainload of fuel every two days, while the nuclear plant would consume less than half of a single carload of fuel per year. With current prices for coal and uranium, this would make the fuel cost of nuclear power about half the fuel cost for coal.

Whether the trade-off of higher construction costs for lower fuel costs is worthwhile depends on the cost of capital and the percent of capacity at which the plant is operated. Safety problems requiring more frequent shutdowns have seriously reduced the percentage of capacity at which nuclear plants have been able to operate. And although environmental regulations have increased the cost of coal-fired plants too, they have had even more of an impact on nuclear plants in that they have increased the difference in construction costs. In addition, we must consider the hidden costs of the nuclear alternative. The most important of these hidden costs are in waste disposal, dismantling, and health and safety issues.

Nuclear power, to be sure, is not unique in posing health and safety hazards. Pro-nuclear writers often point out that coal too has major health and safety problems. The hazards to which coal miners are exposed far exceed those confronted by workers in the nuclear industry, and air pollution is a very real public health hazard in contrast to the largely speculative hazards of low-level radiation or core meltdowns.

The third major alternative to nonrenewable oil and natural gas is represented by solar energy. Even more than in the case of nuclear power, replacing fossil fuels with solar power represents a trade-off of capital investment and operating costs. The system of dams along the Columbia River between Oregon and Washington, for example, although enormously costly to construct, produces electric power at a very efficient operating rate. Unfortunately, few really attractive sites remain in the United States for large-scale hydroelectric projects. For the immediate future, solar prospects appear to consist of small-scale applications that are economical given today's costs and technology and larger-scale applications that cannot yet repay their capital costs but that offer some promise for future development. New materials using nanotechnology thin films are under development. These films have the potential for low-cost and high-efficiency photovoltaic (electric from light) generation.

One of the most controversial aspects of alternative energy sources concerns their net energy costs. Practitioners of the art of net energy analysis attempt to add up all the energy inputs needed to produce a unit of energy output from a given technology to see if more comes out than goes in. If more energy goes in than comes out, a technology clearly cannot be considered an energy "source" in the conventional meaning of the term.

Assignment

1. Read the source text. Following the note outline model provided on the next page, create a note outline for another three paragraphs. Choose the most important or interesting (to you) portions from the source text.
2. From your outline, write a 3-paragraph composition. Your three topics are: coal, nuclear, and solar. Each paragraph should follow the topic/clincher rule; the first sentence (topic) and the last sentence (clincher) should repeat or reflect two to three key words. Indicate by using a highlighter or making bold the key words which are repeated or reflected in the topic and clincher sentences.

Note Outline and Paragraph Models

The paragraph model provided on the next page shows what your first draft might look like after you edit it for structure and style. It contains the six dress-ups and all of the sentence openers. Note that key words in bold in the last (clincher) sentence repeat key words from the first (topic) sentence. By doing this, you make your paragraphs more unified.

The Economics of Alternative Energy

I. alternatives, coal, abundant 　1.　U.S. reserves, 500 yrs. 　2.　mining, capacity, underused 　3.　sulphur dioxide, acid rain 　4.　consider, environment, 　5.　technology, burn, clean Clincher: repeat (or reflect) 2–3 keywords from the topic.	❺While we study the various **alternatives** to oil and gas, it should be remembered that **coal is highly abundant**. ❶We must realize that current U.S. reserves of coal, <u>which</u> are readily accessible, are sufficient to satisfy U.S. energy needs for the next 500 years. ❷With current mining capacity underutilized, the truly powerful pull comes from the <u>enduring and long-lasting</u> supply. ❻Things seem perfect. ❸Unfortunately, sulphur dioxide gas is produced from the burning of coal, and <u>significantly</u> contributes to the production of acid rain. ❸Thoughtfully, we must consider the environment by <u>diligently</u> focusing our innovation on the development of safe and clean technologies for burning coal. ❹Appearing the savior, **coal is highly abundant** in the United States, and this fact should <u>command and move</u> us, <u>because</u> real success comes from having **alternatives**.

Note Outline: The Economics of Alternative Energy
On a separate sheet of paper, together with your teacher, create your note outline for summarizing the rest of this source material.

Style Tools and Examples
Sentence Openers, Part 2 (Levels B & C now, Level A later)

Here are the remaining sentence openers you were wondering about when you read the paragraph model on the previous page:

❹ **"-ing"/"-ed" openers:** This type of sentence always requires a comma. The subject, which begins with a noun/pronoun/article, comes directly after the comma. In the following examples, the subject is italicized.

>**Appearing** over the horizon, *the corporate jet* soared mightily away.
>**Seated** for a moment, *he* sought to rest.

❺ **Adverb clausal opener:** Previously you used an adverb clause in the middle or end of a sentence. You can also begin a sentence with an adverb clause. Note again that a comma is always necessary, and the subject follows it directly.

>**When** he ran away, the army considered him AWOL.
>**While** he wined, dined and caroused, his profits disappeared.

❻ A **VSS** is a very short sentence of five words or less (not a fragment). Writing can often be long, rambling, and monotonous. Use a VSS in every paragraph to grab the reader's attention.

>Work provided one person a savings of $10,000. **He invested it.**
>He sat quietly before the jury. **The judge raised his gavel.**
>**They are saved.**

Practice: Rewrite the #1 sentence as a #4 ("-ing") and as a #5 (clausal) opener:

❶ We will soon see the President face-to-face and hear his policies.

❹ *Seeing the President face-to-face,* _____.

❺ *When we visit the President,* _____.

Practice: Now rewrite the #1 sentence in all six opener patterns:

❶ Those who have savings do not take pleasure in waste, but rejoice in frugality.

❷ _____

_____.

❸ _____

_____ .

❹ _____

_____ .

❺ _____

_____ .

❻ _____

_____ .

Checksheet for Lesson 10

Levels A, B, & C

Presentation
___ title centered and underlined
___ name, date
___ clearly presented

Mechanics
___ indent paragraphs
___ complete sentences
___ capitals (uppercase)
___ punctuation

Structure
___ follows model
___ paragraphs roughly equal size
___ topic and clincher sentences
     repeat or reflect 2-3 key words

Style Tools
___ underline dress-ups (one of each)
___ no "banned" adjectives
___ no "banned" verbs

Sentence Openers (B & C only)
___ ❶ subject
___ ❷ preposition
___ ❸ "-ly" word
___ ❹ "ing"/"ed" opener
___ ❺ adverb clausal opener
___ ❻ VSS (<5 words)

Paragraphs	I.	II.	III.
Level A			
Dress-Ups			
"-ly" word	___	___	___
"who/which" clause	___	___	___
"because" clause	___	___	___
quality adjective	___	___	___
adverb clause			
(www.asia)	___	___	___
strong verb	___	___	___
Level B			
Dress-Ups			
"-ly" word	___	___	___
"who/which" clause	___	___	___
(no "to be" verbs with			
"who/which")	___	___	___
"because" clause	___	___	___
quality adjective	___	___	___
adverbial clause			
(www.asia)	___	___	___
strong verb	___	___	___
sentence openers	___	___	___
(#1, #2, #3, #5)			
Level C			
Dress-Ups			
dual "-ly" word	___	___	___
"who/which" clause	___	___	___
invisible "who/which"			
(no "to be" verbs with	___	___	___
"who/which")			
dual adjectives	___	___	___
adverbial clause	___	___	___
strong verbs	___	___	___
sentence openers	___	___	___
(#1, #2, #3, #5)			

Lesson 11: Three Views of Poverty

Objective

To learn to create outlines by topic, in this case, three paragraphs on one theme—poverty.

Source Text I	Source Text II	Source Text III
Poverty is a matter not so much of low incomes but of how people cope with the fact of having low incomes. Some low-income households honestly, industriously, and successfully make do with what they have, keep families together, and keep children out of trouble. Others, including many that statistically speaking have been raised above the so-called poverty threshold, are for one reason or another unable to cope. They fall into a pattern of social pathologies ranging from juvenile crime and teenage pregnancy to drug and alcohol abuse. They turn newly constructed public housing into instant slums, and in a variety of ways they frustrate the hopes of those who aspire to eliminate poverty through generous public spending and giving. No amount of income redistribution can by itself eliminate poverty. If poorly conceived, *(cont. next pg. col. I)*	The wealthiest 1 percent of the population owns over 40 percent of all capital. The wealthiest 20 percent of U.S. citizens earn over 40 percent of all personal income, while the poorest 20 percent must make do with only 5 percent of the total. Behind these simple statistics lies a whole host of economic policy issues. In the United States today, it is widely accepted that one of the major functions of government is to influence the distribution of income. There is no doubt that poverty exists in the United States despite the fact that its people, by many measures, continue to have the highest average incomes in the world. Poverty is plainly seen in vast neighborhoods in every large city. It is tucked away only slightly less visibly in small towns and rural areas throughout our country. People are poor if they cannot afford the simple necessities of *(cont. next pg. col. II)*	What constitutes low income must be defined in subjective terms, relative to the incomes of others in society. A poverty-level household income should be defined as one equal to less than half of the median income for all households in a given society. So, poverty-level income is really a moving target rather than an objectively defined threshold. Nonetheless, poverty can be overcome by raising the incomes of the poor in proper proportion to the incomes of everybody else in a given society. The reason our government selected an objective, need-based official definition of poverty in the first place was to provide a benchmark against which to measure progress toward the elimination of poverty. On the basis of the official definition, the incidence of poverty fell rapidly during the 1960s—from 22.4 percent of the population in 1959 to 12.1 percent in *(cont. next pg. col. III)*

government programs foster dependency and destroy self-respect, they make things worse. They, in fact, foster the continuance of the cycle of poverty. Efforts to redistribute income are reflected not only in explicit anti-poverty programs but also in the tendency to subject almost every policy decision to the test: What does it do for the poor? Perhaps, we might do more for the poor by helping the entrepreneur, the small businessman; by assisting the creative and innovative forces at work in our economy. These are the engines that drive the future. These are the people who build wealth for our nation. Jobs are created for the jobless, and charitable donations are made possible through an increase in the success rate of small business ventures.	life—food, clothing, and shelter. With government programs, we can raise people up out of poverty by lifting their incomes above an objectively defined poverty threshold. This is the official view of the United States government—and for good reason. This approach begins with the idea of an "economy food plan" devised by the U.S. Department of Agriculture*. The plan calculates the cost of providing a balanced nutritive diet. The cost of the plan varies according to the size of a given family, the age of its members, and their place of residence. Other needs must be satisfied too, so, to take those other needs into account, the government sets the low-income level—the dividing line between the poor and the non-poor— at three times the cost of the "economy food plan." *USDA – CNPP (Thrifty Food Plan).	1969. During the 1970s, 1980s, 1990s, and in the new millennium, there has been essentially no further reduction in the number of officially measured poor families. In fact, certain measurements indicate that the percentages are returning now to the pre-1960s era. Therefore, the government must do something with great haste and effort! The officially defined poverty threshold is not enough. It is time for subjective reasoning to play a part. Objective measurements are only useful to a point. It is imperative to realize that the wealthiest 1 percent of the population owns over 40 percent of all capital, and the wealthiest 20 percent of U.S. citizens earn over 40 percent of all personal income, while the poorest 20 percent must make do with only 5 percent of the total. It is time for aggressive, government-directed redistribution!

Assignment

1. Read the three columns of source text and create a note outline using the space provided. Choose key words from the most interesting or important facts, considering which ones will help you most to build upon the theme of poverty and the controversial economic views.
2. From your outline, write a three-paragraph composition on these three perspectives of poverty. Be sure to follow the checksheet on page 64. Also, remember to follow the topic-clincher rule and to highlight (or make

bold) the key words which are reflecting or repeating.

3. As usual, edit carefully, get a second opinion, and rewrite or type a final draft. Be sure to save your completed composition for use with a later assignment in Unit VIII.

Note Outline: Three Views of Poverty

I.   <u>Problem, ⊘ low income</u>

_____

_____

_____

_____

_____

_____

Clincher

II.   <u>Highest, incomes, worldwide</u>

_____

_____

_____

_____

_____

_____

Clincher

III.   Subjective, relative, others

_____

_____

_____

_____

_____

_____

_____

Clincher

Style Tools and Examples
Strengthening Weak Verbs

Used as main verbs, state of being verbs such as *is, am, are, was,* and *were* weaken your sentences. To avoid state of being verbs, you can often do one of the following: (A) substitute an action verb, (B) change the form (e.g., from an adjective to a verb) of a word, or (C) rewrite the sentence.

(Model) The poor man was ready and willing to go to work.
   (A) The poor man **experienced** tremendous willingness.
   (B) The poor man **willed** his life toward a better paying job.
   (C) Poverty stricken for years, this man longed for meaningful work.

In the following sentences, practice revising state of being verbs. Use each of the ways discussed above.

   1. He **was** never a slave to any government program.

   (A) _____

   (B) _____

   (C) _____

2. The poor people **were** worried because of their hunger.

(A) _____

(B) _____

(C) _____

Sentence Openers (new for Level A, review for Levels B & C) Refer to the preposition list on page 48. Following the examples, rewrite the sentences to include sentence openers #2 and #3. Please use a separate sheet of notebook paper if needed.

(subject)	❶ **The people** saw homeless persons walking the streets.
(preposition)	❷ **From** the comfort of their homes, the people saw homeless persons walking the streets.
("-ly" word)	❸ **Unexpectedly**, the people saw homeless persons walking the streets.

(subject)	❶ The man did not associate his poverty with keeping his family together.
(preposition)	❷ _____
("-ly" word)	❸ _____

(subject)	❶ The businessman reached out to assist the poor through charitable donations.
(preposition)	❷ _____
("-ly" word)	❸ _____

Style Note, Level A
In this assignment, write paragraphs with at least subject, prepositional, and "-ly" openers. Practice until you feel comfortable with these three. When you are confident, add the remaining openers one at a time as guided by your teacher.

Checksheet for Lesson 11

Paragraphs	I.	II.	III.

Levels A, B, & C

Presentation
___ title centered and underlined
___ name, date
___ clearly presented

Mechanics
___ indent paragraphs
___ complete sentences
___ capitals (uppercase)
___ punctuation

Structure
___ follows model
___ paragraphs roughly equal size
___ topic and clincher sentences
    repeat or reflect 2-3 key words
___ title reflects key words of final
    sentence in last paragraph

Style Tools
___ underline dress-ups (one of each)
___ no "banned" adjectives
___ no "banned" verbs

Sentence Openers (as required)
___ ❶ subject
___ ❷ preposition
___ ❸ "-ly" word
___ ❹ "ing"/"ed" opener
___ ❺ adverb clausal opener
___ ❻ VSS (<5 words)

Level A

Dress-Ups
"-ly" word   ___ ___ ___
"who/which" clause   ___ ___ ___
"because" clause   ___ ___ ___
quality adjective   ___ ___ ___
adverb clause
(www.asia)   ___ ___ ___
strong verb   ___ ___ ___
Sentence Openers   ___ ___ ___
(#1, #2, #3)

Level B

Dress-Ups
"-ly" word   ___ ___ ___
"who/which" clause   ___ ___ ___
(no "to be" verbs with
"who/which")   ___ ___ ___
quality adjective   ___ ___ ___
adverbial clause
(www.asia)   ___ ___ ___
strong verb   ___ ___ ___
Sentence Openers   ___ ___ ___
(#1, #2, #3, #5, #6)

Level C

Dress-Ups
dual "-ly" word   ___ ___ ___
"who/which" clause   ___ ___ ___
invisible "who/which"
(no "to be" verbs with
"who/which")   ___ ___ ___
dual adjectives   ___ ___ ___
adverbial clause   ___ ___ ___
dual verbs   ___ ___ ___
Sentence Openers (all)   ___ ___ ___

Stylistic Decorations (Level C)

From now on, include one stylistic decoration in every paragraph. Use them moderately; try not to reuse decorations in a composition. The six decorations are:

Question
Conversation (quotations)
Simile and Metaphor
3sss (three short staccato sentences)
Alliteration
Dramatic paragraph opening and closing

Question

In compositions, questions immediately cause your audience to start wondering what their answers would be, interesting them in what you have to say. Suppose you are writing a composition about guns and gun control. You could effectively grab your reader's attention by writing,

"Should handguns be controlled, licensed, registered, or even banned?"

Or, if you were writing a composition about the importance of knowing a second language, you might begin with the following question,

"In many countries, students are required to learn English as they study their native language. In addition, most of the world recognizes English as the primary international language. Given these facts, why do so many Americans still seek to learn a foreign language?"

Conversation (Quotations)

In a narrative composition, (for example, "The Fox and the Crow") you *could* tell the story without conversation, but a few lines of dialogue would add variety.

The fox sat down and smirked. Putting on his most debonair air, he began, "My dear crow, most gorgeous creature in the woods, I swoon when you sing. Will you please favor me with a tune?"

Quotations also have a place in creative writing. The passage below, taken from Keats' "Ode to a Nightingale", is one of the most profound expressions of loneliness in a strange place.

"Perhaps the self same song that found a path
Through the sad heart of Ruth, when, sick for home,
She stood in tears amid the alien corn."

You can work passages such as this into your own writing. For example,

> *"There I was in the heart of the city—alone, fearful, and hungry. Lost in the traffic I felt like Ruth, homesick, standing 'in tears among the alien corn.' How terribly alien this new city seemed to me."*

You can also use quotations to add to history reports, biographical accounts, and various other assignments.

> *Hitler wrote in the Nazi press: "Never in my life have I been so well disposed and inwardly contented as in these days. For hard reality has opened the eyes of millions of Germans to the unprecedented swindles, lies, and betrayals of the Marxist deceivers of the people."*

Similes and Metaphors

Similes and metaphors draw comparisons between two seemingly unlike or unrelated things. A simile uses *like* or *as*, whereas a metaphor does not.

> *The wind was a torrent of darkness among the gusty trees,*
> *The moon was a ghostly galleon tossed upon cloudy seas,*
> *The road was a ribbon of moonlight over the purple moor.*

In this passage from Alfred Noyes, the wind was not a torrent, the moon was not a galleon (a type of ship), and the road was not a ribbon. They are all metaphors, which could have been converted to similes by adding the word *like* to each line. For instance, "The moon was like a ghostly galleon…"

Try to use metaphors and similes in your writing on a regular basis. In compositions longer than five paragraphs, for example, you could write a simile into one paragraph and a metaphor into another.

Three Short Staccato Sentences (3sss)

Three short sentences provide emphasis and attract the reader's attention, especially if they follow certain patterns, such as 4:4:4 (4 words in each sentence) or 4:3:2. (Each sentence has one word less than the one before it.)

> *Employees approach me. They surround me. They encompass me.*
> *[3:3:3]*

Using 3sss also gives you the opportunity to use an occasional sentence fragment for extra emphasis. Be careful, though; while sentence fragments can be effective, they can also confuse your reader if you overuse them.

Alliteration

Alliteration is the repetition of initial sounds in adjacent words or syllables. Examples of alliteration:

Dust of death   *Down to the dust*   *Ravening and roaring lion (This one is a double alliteration: two sounds repeat, the "r" and the "ing" sounds.)*

Dramatic Paragraph Openings and Closings

The dramatic paragraph opening and closing requires that the topic sentence of the paragraph always comes first in the paragraph—except when you have a dramatic opening of five words or less. The dramatic opening, a VSS, comes just before the topic sentence. The dramatic closing is the last sentence of the paragraph. If your composition is short (up to five paragraphs), when you write in a dramatic opening, you must end with a dramatic closing. Later, in larger compositions, you can use a dramatic opening or closing alone in the paragraph.

"Here I am, boss." Faithfully, the manager answered the boss' call and humbly set out with his newly hired employees toward success.
(Paragraph Details Here)
Answering the boss' call, the manager faithfully and humbly led his firm to market growth while making a fair profit. This man truly served the Shareholders well.

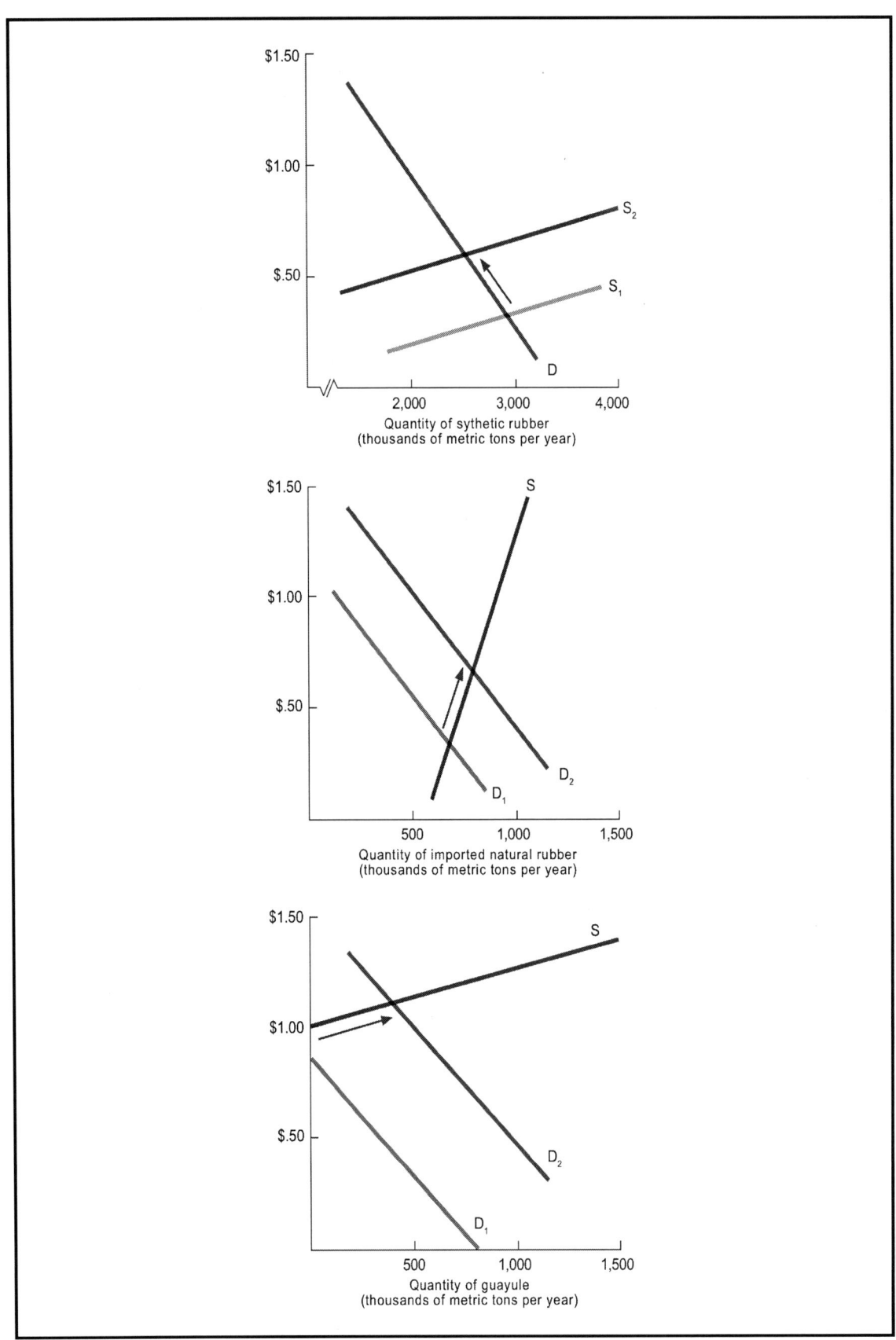

Quantity of sythetic rubber
(thousands of metric tons per year)

Quantity of imported natural rubber
(thousands of metric tons per year)

Quantity of guayule
(thousands of metric tons per year)

Unit V: Writing Stories From Pictures
Lesson 12: Can Guayule Bounce Back?

Objective
To practice writing a composition within the framework provided by three pictures and a source text.

Source Text

Please refer to the three pictures (graphs) on page 68. These are supply and demand graphs. In order to understand supply and demand graphs you must first understand the concept of equilibrium. Equilibrium is the price point at which the supply line intersects the demand line. Only if people are willing to pay that price, or higher, are producers motivated to supply. If the supply line and demand line do not intersect, then the maximum price people are willing to pay is too low to motivate production. This is the case pictured in the third graph where current demand is represented by the line D_1. Only if demand would increase to a level like the one represented by line D_2, at a price above \$1.00 per pound, would producers be willing to supply any reasonable tonnage of natural rubber sourced from the scruffy native American desert plant "Guayule" (pronounced why-oo-lee).

Right behind oil, rubber is the second largest item on the U.S. import bill each year. Rubber can either be supplied from synthetic conversion of petroleum, or it can be sourced from a plant, most commonly the rubber tree plant. However, most rubber is made from petroleum. Graph number one shows that supply has been about 2,900,000 tons per year at the equilibrium price of \$.30 per pound (S_1.) However, because synthetic rubber is made from petroleum, production costs have skyrocketed in recent years. This is shown as a shift in the synthetic rubber supply curve from S_1 to S_2. At the new equilibrium price of \$.60 per pound, people are only willing to buy about 2,500,000 tons per year.

Guayule, rich in natural rubber, has contributed nothing at all in recent years. But it was not always so. Guayule supplied elastic balls for the Aztecs. It supplied half of U.S. rubber needs during the early 1900s. And 32,000 acres of Guayule were planted in America during World War II, when the Japanese cut off supplies of natural rubber from Asian rubber tree plants. Guayule entrepreneurs think the plant is now set to "bounce back."

The second graph shows what has happened in the market for Asian tree rubber. Because synthetic rubber and natural rubber are substitutes, the increase in the price of the synthetic product has pushed the demand curve for imported natural rubber to the right ($D_1 \rightarrow D_2$). As a result, the demand shift for natural rubber has pushed the price up sharply to about \$.70 per pound. At the old equilibrium price of \$.30 per pound, people bought about 700,000 tons of natural rubber each year. At the new equilibrium price of \$.70 per pound, people buy about 800,000 tons/year. You can imagine that the growers of Asian rubber trees are very happy about high oil prices! But it's not just the high oil prices driving this market. In addition, certain newer products require the use of at least some natural rubber. Radial tires, for example, cannot be made exclusively from synthetic rubber.

Other newer products, like hypoallergenic rubber products, require the use of specialized natural rubber sources. The latex which comes from Asian tree rubber can cause some people to have an allergic reaction. Guayule rubber does not cause any allergic reaction. There are synthetic alternatives for medical device products, but they are just not as stretchy as natural rubber. Guayule performs like Asian tree rubber but contains none of the proteins that cause latex allergies. In April 2008, the U.S. Food and Drug Administration cleared for marketing the first device made from Guayule rubber, the Yulex Patient Examination Glove.

What if oil prices go up even higher in the future? Perhaps happy Guayule entrepreneurs will be supplying 400,000 tons/year at $1.10 per pound (See D_2 – graph three.) What do you think will happen? Will we recycle more old rubber?

Assignment

1. Read the source text.
2. Carefully examine the series of pictures (graphs) corresponding to this assignment. Determine key words to help you make a topic sentence for each paragraph which reflects the central fact of the picture. Ask questions of yourself to fill in the details, based on the picture, the source text, and your ideas about what might be happening with the supply and demand of rubber.
3. Write a 3-paragraph composition, correlating the pictures and the written account. Use the checklist, and be sure to underline dress-ups, and mark sentence openers with numbers in the margin (or in brackets if typed). Level C students should also include one decoration in each paragraph, and put *dec* in the margin on the line where it occurs.

Structural Tools and Suggestions
Using a Picture's Central Fact
At all levels, the key introduction should be the topic sentence (the first in the paragraph). The clincher sentence (the last in the paragraph) should repeat or reflect 2–3 key words from the topic sentence.

The only element that must be mentioned is the central fact of the picture. Level B & C students will develop more facts and ideas beyond what is obviously seen in the picture.

Extracting Details from the Picture
Some people are better at seeing a picture and thinking of ways to describe it or things to say about it. One technique to help come up with the content is to ask

yourself questions about the portrayed image. The answers to your questions then become the details for your outline. As you begin writing from your outline, more ideas will flow. Adding dress-ups and sentence openers will also help you to add detail. Some questions that may be helpful include:

Who or What is in the picture?
Why is this situation happening?
When did this begin, or what happened just before this picture?
Where exactly is this, or what might be just outside this picture?
How is this being done?
What might happen after this picture?

Become a master at asking questions about pictures. The ability to ask oneself questions and hear answers is the core skill required for all creative writing and thinking. Practice asking questions constantly. Level B & C students will derive detail and further elaboration from simple pictures by asking these questions. Especially questions like, "What might be just outside this picture? What might happen right after this picture? What did happen just before this picture?"

Although the series of pictures might tell a story of sorts, it doesn't necessarily have to. Think of this model as "event description", where the topic sentence tells what's happening, and the rest of the paragraph explains what's going on in the minds of the participants and what's happening behind the scenes. It is a creative unit, so feel free to imagine what might have been, and have fun with it.

Style Tools and Examples
"-ing"/ "-ed" openers (new for Level A, review for Levels B & C)

A sentence that begins with an "-ing" or "-ed" opener *must* have a comma directly before the subject. Study the examples below where sentences that begin with ordinary subject openers get transformed into stronger sentences with an "-ing" or "-ed" opener. Subjects are in italics and commas appear before them. By using an "-ing" or "-ed" opener, you can also avoid weak verbs such as *is, am, are, was,* and *were*. Remember, when you use sentence openers in your compositions, put the number *4* in the margin.

1. (Model) The boy was jogging along the road and spied a deer. ▶
   Jogging along the road, *the boy* spied a deer.
2. (Model) The entrepreneur was taking a chance and bet on Guayule. ▶
   Taking a chance, *the entrepreneur* bet on Guayule.
3. (Model) She was trembling with fear and approached the banker. ▶
   Trembling with fear, *she* approached the banker.

Practice: Convert the following into an "-ing" or "-ed" opener, remembering the comma.

71

1. Jim was thoughtful after the investor's visit and felt grateful for his staff. ▶

---

2. John was traveling to Washington D.C. to represent his party. ▶

---

3. People were gathered around the computer and watched in wonder. ▶

More Style Tools and Examples
Punctuating Lists

Often, writers need to list several items in one sentence. It is important to use commas properly to avoid confusion. Structure your lists following the examples below.

Three items:	Rubber companies, Indian tribes, and agribusiness concerns are all planting experimental plots.
Four items:	George built a house, purchased Guayule seeds, gathered food and medicine, and waited for the funds to rain in.
Five items:	Chris developed a business based on creativity, productivity, enthusiasm, service, and commitment.

Using Commas with Lists

There exists a difference of opinion in how commas should be used when listing similar items. Twentieth century American punctuation seems to lean toward using a comma after a second item in a list and before the conjunction, as in:

He ate apples, oranges, and pears.

This is generally referred to as the "Oxford" comma, or less commonly the "Harvard" comma, which came about because both Oxford University Press and Harvard University Press favor it. Technically, it is called the "serial" comma. The argument in favor of the second comma in a list of three things is that it often helps reduce ambiguity, which can be seen in statements such as this book dedication:

To my parents, Ayn Rand and God.

Ultimately, whether you should use the second comma or not depends on clarity, your publisher or your teacher, and your personal preference. Be consistent throughout your document.

Outline: Can Guayule Bounce Back?

I. Central fact:

1. _____

2. _____

3. _____

4. _____

5. _____

Clincher

II. Central fact:

1. _____

2. _____

3. _____

4. _____

5. _____

Clincher

III. Central fact:

1. _____

2. _____

3. _____

4. _____

5. _____

Clincher

Checksheet for Lesson 12

Paragraphs	I.	II.	III.

Levels A, B, & C

Presentation
___ title centered and underlined
___ name, date
___ clearly presented

Mechanics
___ indent paragraphs
___ complete sentences
___ capitals (uppercase)
___ punctuation

Structure
___ follows model
___ paragraphs roughly equal size
___ topic and clincher sentences
 repeat or reflect 2-3 key words
___ title reflects key words of final
 sentence in last paragraph

Style Tools
___ underline dress-ups (one of each)
___ no "banned" adjectives
___ no "banned" verbs

Sentence Openers (as required)
___ ❶ subject
___ ❷ preposition
___ ❸ "-ly" word
___ ❹ "ing"/ "ed" opener
___ ❺ adverb clausal opener
___ ❻ VSS (<5 words)

Level A

 Dress-Ups
 "-ly" word ___ ___ ___
 "who/which" clause ___ ___ ___
 "because" clause ___ ___ ___
 quality adjective ___ ___ ___
 adverb clause
 (www.asia) ___ ___ ___
 strong verb ___ ___ ___
Sentence Openers ___ ___ ___
 (#1, #2, #3)

Level B

 Dress-Ups
 "-ly" word ___ ___ ___
 "who/which" clause ___ ___ ___
 (no "to be" verbs with
 "who/which")
 dual adjective ___ ___ ___
 adverbial clause
 (www.asia) ___ ___ ___
 strong verb ___ ___ ___
Sentence Openers (all) ___ ___ ___

Level C

 Dress-Ups
 dual "-ly" word ___ ___ ___
 "who/which" clause ___ ___ ___
 invisible "who/which"
 (no "to be" verbs with
 "who/which") ___ ___ ___
 dual adjectives ___ ___ ___
 adverbial clause ___ ___ ___
 dual verbs ___ ___ ___
Sentence Openers (all) ___ ___ ___
Decoration (one/paragraph) ___ ___ ___

Unit VI: Research Reports
Lesson 13: How to Plan a Business

Objective
To begin to understand the complexities of writing from multiple sources, and to introduce the fused outline.

Source Texts

Source 1	Source 2
In order to plan a business, one must create a business plan. Too many businesses make business plans only when they have to. Unless the bank or the investors want a plan, there is no plan. "Not enough time for a plan," entrepreneurs say. "I can't plan. I'm too busy getting things done."	The Executive Summary should appear at the front of any excellent business plan. Although it appears at the front, it should be the last portion of the plan to be written. A proper Executive Summary should be no more than just a page or two recapitulating the highlights of your plan.
The busier you are, the more you need to plan. If you are always putting out fires, you should build fire breaks or put in a sprinkler system. You can lose the whole forest for too much attention to the trees.	Following the Executive Summary, the next portion of your plan should be titled "Company Description." In this section you will describe the legal establishment, the history, and your start-up plans.
Business plans don't sell new business ideas to venture capitalists. The plan, though it is necessary, is only one way to present information. Venture capitalists invest in people and ideas. Your business plan is no substitute for these!	Thirdly, describe your Product or Service. This is the section where you describe what you are selling. In this section, it is imperative that you focus upon customer benefits.
	Market Analysis is your fourth section. It is extremely important that you know your market, customer needs, customer locations, and how to reach them.
Don't use a business plan to show how much you know about your business. Use it to set concrete tasks, responsibilities, and deadlines. Use it to guide your business. All businesses, not just new businesses or large corporations, need business planning. A business plan sets goals and priorities, providing a forum for regular review and course corrections. *(cont.)*	The fifth section is for Strategy and Implementation. Be specific. You must include management responsibilities with dates and budgets. Make sure you can track results and adjust when necessary. *(cont.)*

If things don't work out exactly as planned after completion of the first business year, then spend time reviewing the original assumption of your plan. Perhaps the market is different than you first imagined. Maybe new opportunities are waiting just ahead if you stop to reassess and set a new, adjusted course of action. The plan must be flexible!

Even though it's flexible, that is no excuse for not performing to plan. In fact, you can use a "balanced score card" with the "management by objectives" approach. With these tools, you will tie each employee's salary, bonus, and stock options to key objectives which serve the greater, overall business plan objectives.

The Web Plan Summary comes next. For e-commerce, it is important to include a discussion of your website, development costs, operations, and sales and marketing strategies.

The seventh portion of your business plan should describe your Management Team. The reader needs to understand your organization and the key management team members involved.

Finally, Financial Analysis completes any well-prepared plan. Cash flow is the single most important numerical analysis in a business plan, and should never be missing. Most business plans should also have a sales forecast and a profit and loss statement with projections over time. In addition, all business plans should contain a projected (proforma) balance sheet, business ratios, and complete market analysis tables.

Assignment

1. Read each source, noting that there appears to be some factual and interpretational differences between them. How is a researcher to deal with interpretational differences?
2. You, the researcher, must weigh the evidence and determine what to present to your audience. It is important to develop your abilities of discernment and skill in handling discrepancies.
3. Study the outlines below. Notes were taken from Source 1, additional notes from Source 2. Some of the facts were the same or similar; some appear in one source but not the other. The chart on the right shows which details were used in the "fused" outline. Creating a chart such as this may be helpful for you as you take the notes and create the fused outline in the next two lessons.
4. Write a three-paragraph composition using the fused outline provided, or adjusting it to your preferences. Follow the checksheet on page 79. As always, create your first draft, edit, and rewrite or type a final copy.

Style Tools and Suggestions (all levels)

Similar to previous lessons, you may need to elaborate on the events, including details that are not explicitly stated in the source texts. You may not, however, feel comfortable if you think you are "adding facts". In this case where you need to make a supposition or assumption about what someone thought or said, you may find that "-ly" words such as *possibly, probably, presumably,* and *likely* would allow you some freedom to infer and describe details without changing or adding anything. In Units IV and VI, we are not really "telling a story" like we did in Units III and V; we are telling about—or reporting on—events and facts. Therefore, we can use objective expressions like these to add detail without claiming any authority to know what is not directly written.

> "One might imagine how…"   "We could suppose that…"

Notes and Fused Outline Models: How to Plan a Business

The fused outline incorporates details from the note outlines you make from your sources. First, create note outlines for each paragraph of your sources. Then, review your outlines and choose details that you want to include in your report. In your fused outline, keep the number of details equal throughout your topics.

Note Outline: Source 1 / Source 2	Fused Outline	From Source 1	From Source 2

Note Outline: Source 1
- Some entrepreneurs don't plan
- The busier you are the more you need a plan
- But the plan is no substitute for excellent people and ideas
- Use your plan to set concrete tasks, responsibilities, and deadlines
- Be ready to make course corrections as needed
- The plan must always be flexible
Note Outline: Source 2
- Executive Summary appears first but prepared last
- Describe the company
- Describe the product or service—focus on the customer
- Analyze the market
- Strategy and Implementation
- Make sure you can track results and adjust as needed
- Web Plan Summary
- Management Team
- Financials with cash flow, proforma balance sheet/ P&L, and sales forecast
	I. Some entrepreneurs don't plan—say they're too busy
	  1. Busier you are/more a plan is needed
	  2. No substituting for great people and ideas
	  3. Make people productive
	Clincher
	II. Business Plan Structure
	  1. Executive Summary
	  2. Company Description
	  3. Product or Service
	  4. Market Analysis
	  5. Strategy & Implementation
	  6. Web Plan Summary
	  7. Management Team
	  8. Financial Analysis
	Clincher
	III. Always Flexible but Results Oriented
	  1. Course Corrections
	  2. Adjust tasks, responsibility, and deadlines
	  3. Management by Objectives
	Clincher
		√
		√
		√
		√
		
		√ √
		√
		
		√
			
			√
			
			√
			√
			√
			√
			√
			√
			√
			√
			
			√

Research Tools and Suggestions

Research, at its simplest, is the combination of two sources to create a third; this involves gathering materials such as facts, figures, and opinions from many sources to create a new theory or interpretation. A source is any place where you obtain information (i.e., books, magazines, videos, newspapers, and the Internet). As you practice research, you will learn to fuse multiple interpretations to draw a larger truth or to point out the differences between your sources.

Style Tools and Examples
Level C: Adjectival Teeter-totters

To make an adjectival "teeter-totter", place the dual adjectives dress-up just before the noun and the who/which clause after it. The noun forms the fulcrum of the teeter-totter. When you include this technique in your composition, the adjectives and who/which it uses will count as the minimum dress-up for the checklist.

1.   (Model) The weary old **hunter** who climbed the hill sat a moment to rest.
                                      ∧

2.   (Model) His young and trusting **son** who carried the gun stood by.
                                    ∧

Practice:

3.   The _____(and/but/,) _____ **pair** who
                                              ∧
_____, had faith in their business plan.

4.   The owners gave the businessman a _____ (and/but/,)

_____ **test** which _____.
              ∧

5.   Suddenly there arose a _____(and/but/,)

_____ **wind** which _____.
                ∧

78

Checksheet for Lessons 13 & 14

	Paragraphs	I.	II.	III.

Levels A, B, & C

Presentation
___ title centered and underlined
___ name, date
___ clearly presented

Mechanics
___ indent paragraphs
___ complete sentences
___ capitals (uppercase)
___ punctuation

Structure
___ follows model
___ paragraphs roughly equal size
___ topic and clincher sentences
       repeat or reflect 2-3 key words
___ title reflects key words of final
       sentence in last paragraph

Style Tools
___ underline dress-ups (one of each)
___ sentence openers marked
___ no "banned" adjectives
___ no "banned" verbs

Sentence Openers (as required)
___ ❶ subject
___ ❷ preposition
___ ❸ "-ly" word
___ ❹ "ing"/ "ed" opener
___ ❺ adverb clausal opener
___ ❻ VSS (<5 words)

Level A

Dress-Ups
"-ly" word   ___ ___ ___
"who/which" clause   ___ ___ ___
quality adjective   ___ ___ ___
adverb clause
(www.asia)   ___ ___ ___
 strong verb   ___ ___ ___
Sentence Openers   ___ ___ ___
 (#3, #4, #6)

Level B

Dress-Ups
"-ly" word   ___ ___ ___
"who/which" clause   ___ ___ ___
 invisible "who/which"   ___ ___ ___
dual adjective   ___ ___ ___
adverbial clause
(www.asia)   ___ ___ ___
 dual verbs   ___ ___ ___
Sentence Openers (all)   ___ ___ ___

Level C

Dress-Ups
dual "-ly" word   ___ ___ ___
adjectival "teeter-totter" ___ ___ ___
invisible "who/which"   ___ ___ ___
(no "to be" verbs with
"who/which")
adverbial clause   ___ ___ ___
dual verbs   ___ ___ ___
Sentence Openers (all)   ___ ___ ___
Decoration (one/paragraph) ___ ___ ___

Lesson 14: The Politics of Global Warming

Objective
To practice writing research reports from multiple sources. In this exercise there are three sources; you should try to use all of them.

Source Texts

A.	B.	C.
The chasm between rich and poor on how to address climate change took center stage at a recent G-8 summit. It will be difficult to persuade the world to make the lifestyle and economic sacrifices needed to save the planet from global warming. The two budding powers, India and China, that are just now getting comfortable economically, demonstrate the greatest reluctance to change. The President said that the United States had a "historic responsibility" to take the lead in emissions reduction efforts because the U.S. still has a larger carbon footprint than developing nations. He went on to say, "I know that in the past, the United States has sometimes fallen short of meeting our responsibilities. So, let me be clear: those days are over!" But, he also said, "With most of the growth in projected emissions coming from developing countries, their active participation is a prerequisite for a solution." However, negotiations have made no major breakthrough on firm commitments to reduce carbon emissions. Significantly, the Group of	For too long, we have disguised the cost of one of our most destructive activities: emitting pollution that is making the earth warmer. We have allowed this by making the market price of emitting those pollutants zero. This must now stop! In 2009, outside of New York City's Madison Square Garden, a "mega-meter" of sorts on human-caused climate change was unveiled. The 67-by-32-foot electronic billboard monitors in realtime the cumulative pollution humans are emitting into the earth's atmosphere. You can view it on the Internet at: know-the-number.com This "carbon counter" is no gimmick. It is based upon cutting-edge climate change science, with actual emissions being updated every tenth of a second by MIT scientists. Behavioral economists will tell you that the simple act of placing an electricity consumption meter in plain view can substantially cut a home's energy use. When people are allowed to see their	Global warming is a complete falsehood, fabricated for political reasons. All the worry is about CO_2. But human activity on our planet is not the main source of CO_2. Volcanoes, animals, bacteria, decaying vegetation, and the oceans produce a lot more. There really is nothing new about global warming. During the era of the dinosaur, our planet was warmer, the sea level was higher, there were no polar ice caps, and we had one super-continent called Pangaea. Then there was the Great Ice Age, around 2 million years ago, when tremendous ice sheets sucked up and lowered sea level by approximately 450 feet below the current level. That, unmistakably, is a climate change, and there were no human activities to induce it. Contrary to the insistence of the mainstream press and career bureaucrats, there is no scientific consensus on "global warming" or that—if it exists at all—it is caused by human activity.

A.	B.	C.
Eight made no firm commitment to help developing countries financially cope with the effects of rising seas, increased droughts and floods, or to provide the technology to make their carbon-heavy economies more climate-friendly. The Kyoto Protocol will expire in 2012.	real-time consumption of power, they are then motivated to conserve. If the price of costly activities isn't hidden from us, we are more likely to pursue those activities prudently.	According to the free-market environment organization PERC (Political Economy Research Center) in Bozeman, Montana, a majority of climate scientists have never endorsed the notion that human activity is causing global warming or that warming is a crisis that requires immediate urgent action.

Assignment

1. Using the format taught in Lesson 13, take notes on each source so that you have three note outlines.
2. From your note outlines, create a fused outline. Place checkmarks (√) showing from which source each note came. Put the fused outline in the space provided on page 87. This report outline should have one Roman numeral and *not more than* five details for each paragraph. Lesson 13 presented an anomaly since there were eight details required in the second paragraph to provide a complete description of the elements contained within a comprehensive business plan.
3. Following your report outline, write a 3-paragraph report. Refer to the checksheet on page 79.
4. Review your first draft, adding any dress-ups and sentence openers you missed, and editing for improvements. Have it checked, then handwrite or type a final copy for your portfolio.

Note Outline

Source A: _____

1. _____

2. _____

3. _____

4. _____

5. _____

Source B: _____

1. _____

2. _____

3. _____

4. _____

5. _____

Source C: _____

1. _____

2. _____

3. _____

4. _____

5. _____

Fused Outline

I. Global Warming?

1. _____

2. _____

3. _____

4. _____

5. _____

Clincher

II. Can We Motivate Change?

1. _____

2. _____

3. _____

4. _____

5. _____

Clincher

III. Should We Motivate Change?

1. _____

2. _____

3. _____

4. _____

5. _____

Clincher

Lesson 15: Hard Times

Objective
To practice writing research reports from multiple sources, and adding in your own idea, opinion, perception or belief.

Source Texts

A.	B.
In 2009, many families began cooking dinner instead of going out to eat and renting movies instead of trekking to the multiplex. Families across the nation began making trade-offs because of the economy. When a parent is laid off, even tougher financial choices are required. For example, can we keep paying for piano lessons? Can we afford a family vacation? Can we still afford college?	In 2009, leaders of the G-8, plus five of the fastest developing nations, called for open markets and a battle against protectionism as the answer to the world's economic meltdown. But the need to save jobs back home pulled them in the opposite direction. How do we balance between global economic recovery and the pressure to protect local industries and jobs at home?
What did the government do to help? A $787 billion stimulus bill was approved by Congress containing a "Buy American" provision. That means stimulus money can only be used for projects in which all the iron, steel, and manufactured goods are produced in the United States. This protectionist step was really necessary. The hope was that parents who were laid off might find work once again.	The economic crisis stoked protectionist impulses and forced governments, especially the United States, to intervene in the private sector in extraordinary ways. Trade experts said that the steps taken during this crisis didn't approach the protectionist policies that helped cause the Great Depression of the 1930s. But, could another Great Depression be looming? Then, governments including the United States sought to protect domestic businesses and farmers by blocking imports. Other countries did the same and world trade almost came to a total standstill.
When times are tough, what else can parents do? They can share financial values with children, like having a rainy day fund. A recessionary economy can be used as a wonderful example of why it is so important to save. Taking kids grocery shopping with coupons and putting the savings in a piggy bank, eating leftovers and brown-bagging lunches, repairing shoes instead of replacing them—these are all ways	All governments dealing with hard economic times are always under enormous pressure and do well if they can simply resist too much protectionism. When the macroeconomic stress is enormous—it is unlikely to find ways to liberalize trade.

A.	B.
to teach kids the value of a dollar and the importance of being frugal. Economic downturns and financial hardships are going to happen again and again. Parents are their children's primary financial role models. They should not attempt to shield children from these microeconomic realities.	Economic downturns and financial hardships are going to happen again and again. How individuals insulate themselves and deal with hardship is very important for the economy and its recovery. Microeconomic actions in the home and on the job will impact the overall macroeconomic stresses which direct government actions.

Assignment

1. Your ultimate aim is to write a two-paragraph report using the two sources above and following the steps as outlined below.
2. As you read the two source texts, look for the two main topics available in the text (probably "microeconomic" and "macroeconomic" realities like "living in a typical household" and "protectionism," respectively.)
3. Make two note outlines for each of the two topics, taking 3–5 details from each account. (If the lines provided here are not large enough, use extra blank paper.)
4. From the notes, create a two-paragraph fused outline.
5. Following your fused outline, write up the report. Double-space your first draft.
6. Follow the topic/clincher rule and use the checklist provided to continue practice of your stylistic techniques.
7. Proofread your composition, following your checksheet, and get a second opinion.
8. Write or type your final draft, keeping it in your portfolio.

Structural Tools and Suggestions

In your second paragraph, which will likely focus on protectionism, you will certainly want to report the factual details, but you should also include a statement or two about the significance of this macroeconomic reality. This would mean that you are specifically adding in your own idea, opinion, perception or belief. This is perfectly acceptable. Since your name is on the top of your paper under the title, the reader will see that this is your work, and there is no need to say in your report, "I think...", or "I believe that..." or "In my opinion..." Just say what you think, almost like it was another fact. Qualifying your opinion with "I think..." and similar comments, is not only unnecessary, it weakens your writing. If you practice inserting one or two statements of commentary with your facts right now, essay writing (where you will have an entire concluding paragraph with your own ideas and opinions) will be much easier.

Source Outlines, topic one
Source A
Economic Situation:

1. _____

2. _____

3. _____

4. _____

5. _____

Source B
Economic Situation:

1. _____

2. _____

3. _____

4. _____

5. _____

Source Outlines, topic two
Source A
Protectionism:

1. _____

2. _____

3. _____

4. _____

5. _____

Source B
Protectionism:

1. _____

2. _____

3. _____

4. _____

5. _____

Fused Outline, topic one

I. _____

1. _____

2. _____

3. _____

4. _____

5. _____

6. _____

7. _____
Clincher

Fused Outline, topic two

I. _____

1. _____

2. _____

3. _____

4. _____

5. _____

6. _____

7. _____
Clincher

Checksheet for Lesson 15

	Paragraphs	I.	II.

Levels A, B, & C

Presentation
___ title centered and underlined
___ name, date
___ clearly presented

Mechanics
___ indent paragraphs
___ complete sentences
___ capitals (uppercase)
___ punctuation

Structure
___ follows model
___ topic and clincher sentences
    repeat or reflect 2–3 key words
___ title reflects key words of final
    sentence in last paragraph

Style Tools
___ underline dress-ups (one of each)
___ sentence openers marked
___ no "banned" adjectives
___ no "banned" verbs

Sentence Openers (as required)
___ ❶ subject
___ ❷ preposition
___ ❸ "-ly" word
___ ❹ "ing"/"ed" opener
___ ❺ adverb clausal opener
___ ❻ VSS (<5 words)

Level A

  Dress-Ups
  "-ly" word   ___ ___
  "who/which" clause   ___ ___
  quality adjective   ___ ___
  adverb clause
  (www.asia)   ___ ___
   strong verb   ___ ___
Sentence Openers (#3, #4, #6)   ___ ___

Level B

  Dress-Ups
  dual "-ly" word   ___ ___
  "who/which" clause   ___ ___
  invisible "who/which"   ___ ___
  dual adjective   ___ ___
  adverbial clause
  (www.asia)   ___ ___
  dual verbs   ___ ___
Sentence Openers (all)   ___ ___

Level C

  Dress-Ups
  dual "-ly" word   ___ ___
  adjectival "teeter-totter"   ___ ___
  invisible "who/which"   ___ ___
  (no "to be" verbs with
  "who/which")   ___ ___
  adverbial clause   ___ ___
  dual verbs   ___ ___
Sentence Openers (all)   ___ ___
Decoration (one/paragraph)   ___ ___

Unit VII: Creative Writing
Lesson 16: Think and Grow Rich

Objective
To practice taking a topic and, using your imagination, creating a description or narrative.

When you contemplate creative descriptive writing, you must first think: what are some possible themes (topics)? For example, if someone asked you to write on a vacation you recently took, you might ask yourself what topics could possibly form your body paragraphs: 1) location, 2) who you were with, 3) traveling there, 4) food, and 5) what you did. Once you have a list of possible topics, you must choose three, for example: location, who, and what you did.

Then you could easily write a three-paragraph composition, the first paragraph with a topic and clincher using the "location" as a key word, the second paragraph talking about "who" vacationed with you, and the third paragraph explaining "what you did" on your vacation. To make the composition more complete, you would then add in an introduction and a conclusion.

Structural Tools and Suggestions
Introductions
A good introduction offers some background on the topic mentioned in the title and suggests what the reader might expect to find in the composition. The introduction (or introductory paragraph) should:
1. Be the same length as your other body paragraphs.
2. Indicate time and place.
3. Have one or two sentences of historical background on the subject.
4. State the three themes (topics).
5. End with the title.
6. Conform to all the rules of style as in body paragraphs.
7. Not have a topic or clincher sentence.

Conclusions
Conclusions should be one paragraph in length, approximately the same size as all the other paragraphs in the composition. In style they also conform to the body paragraphs. Just as in the introduction, they do not need topic sentences, and it is good to end the conclusion with key words from the title. Your conclusions should:
1. Repeat the three themes (topics).
2. Tell what is most important and why.
3. Tell which is least important and why.
4. End with the title.
5. Never use *I* or *we.*

Conclusions reveal the writer as no other paragraph does. What you decide is "most important" and why you decide it is most important reveal yourself as a writer. Sometimes, what you think is most important, someone else might feel is less important or even irrelevant. There is no right or wrong in creative writing; just be able to justify your choice.

Especially in descriptive creative writing, the key to good organization is "think three themes." Try to fit your ideas into three themes. We'll work on the body paragraphs later. From now on, give your composition an introductory paragraph, three body paragraphs, and a concluding paragraph.

Source Text

The owner of a diner in a small town was faced with the same choices that many business owners have faced in hard times, a loss of income that requires reducing expenses. This owner saw two options: Lay off two employees, or ask every worker to work one day a week without pay. The latter choice would mean that everyone could keep his job—yes, with a day's less wages but without any one person losing all of his wages. Since it seemed like a win-win choice, the employees chose that option.

Word spread around town. Residents discovered which day the employees would work without pay. Something wonderful happened. Town residents decided to eat at the diner on that day and left tips that totaled more than the owner saved by cutting wages and more than the workers lost in pay. Everyone benefited from these choices. Most wonderful of all, the owner and the employees had no idea that the town's people would respond in this way. They made their choice simply because they were grateful to keep their jobs and help each other out. By making the choice they did, everyone gained more than any one person had expected.

Assignment

Write a 5-paragraph creative composition with an introduction, 3-paragraph body, and a conclusion describing the reaction of the town's people. While you will make up most of your composition, include facts given in the source text.

THINK of possible THEMES (topics).

While you can choose any three themes you wish, here are some ideas if you get stuck:
1. The reaction in an ordinary family home.
2. The results of unity (pulling together) for the common good.
3. Is growing rich only about money?
4. How many ways are there to grow rich?

If we take what is available and work together, not only will there be enough; instead there will be abundance! This composition is your creation. Use your imagination, but make sure you organize your ideas into three themes. Each one will take up an entire paragraph. Refer to the checksheet on page 92 to make sure you include all the style and structural elements required of your level.

Model Chart ▶
 	
Because this unit requires you to "create" the ideas, you must get most of your ideas out of your brain. To do this, it is helpful to aggressively ask yourself questions:
 	
WHO? WHAT? WHERE?
WHEN? WHY? HOW? BEST?
WORST? PROBLEMS?
	I. Introduction
	
	  1. Get attention of reader
	  2. Background (time, place)
	  3. State 3 themes (topics)
	
	II. Topic
	        Details
	        Clincher
	
	III. Topic
	        Details
	        Clincher
	
	IV. Topic
	        Details
	        Clincher
	
	V. Conclusion
	    Restate 3 themes (topics)
	    Most significant & why

Creative Writing Procedure for 5-Paragraph Descriptive Composition

Step 1: Determine subject.

Step 2: List possible topics. (Ask yourself questions.)

Step 3: Choose 3 topics; determine order.

Step 4: Create outline and details.

Step 5: Write the body (topic) paragraphs.

Step 6: Write the introduction & conclusion paragraphs.

Checksheet for Lessons 16 & 17

Levels A, B, & C

Presentation
____ title centered and underlined
____ name, date
____ clearly presented

Mechanics
____ indent paragraphs
____ complete sentences
____ capitals (uppercase)
____ punctuation

Structure
____ follows model
____ paragraphs roughly equal size
____ topic and clincher sentences
(BODY PARAGRAPHS ONLY)
____ repeat or reflect 2–3 key words
____ title reflects key words of final sentence in Conclusion **or** last sentence of Introduction

Style Tools
____ underline dress-ups (one of each)
____ no "banned" adjectives
____ no "banned" verbs

Sentence Openers
____ ❶ subject
____ ❷ preposition
____ ❸ "-ly" word
____ ❹ "ing"/ "ed" opener
____ ❺ adverb clausal opener
____ ❻ VSS (<5 words)

Introduction   I.
     time, place, historical background ____
     three themes (topics) ____
     ends with title ____
     stylistic techniques at your level ____

Paragraphs	I.	II.	III.	IV.	V.
Level A					
Dress-Ups					
"-ly" word	____	____	____	____	____
"who/which" clause	____	____	____	____	____
quality adjective	____	____	____	____	____
adverb clause (www.asia)	____	____	____	____	____
strong verb	____	____	____	____	____
Sentence Openers	____	____	____	____	____
Level B					
Dress-Ups					
dual "-ly" words	____	____	____	____	____
"who/which" clause	____	____	____	____	____
invisible "who/which"	____	____	____	____	____
dual adjectives	____	____	____	____	____
adverbial clause	____	____	____	____	____
dual verb	____	____	____	____	____
Sentence Openers	____	____	____	____	____
Decoration	____	____	____	____	____
Level C					
Dress-Ups					
dual "-ly" word	____	____	____	____	____
"who/which" clause	____	____	____	____	____
invisible "who/which"	____	____	____	____	____
adj. "teeter-totter"	____	____	____	____	____
adverbial clause	____	____	____	____	____
dual verbs	____	____	____	____	____
Sentence Openers	____	____	____	____	____
Decoration	____	____	____	____	____

Conclusion   V.
     Repeats three themes (topics) ____
     Most important? Why? ____
     Least important? Why? ____
     Stylistic techniques (at your level) ____

Lesson 17: Hitler's Economic Opportunity

Objective

To practice creative writing as well as designing and writing introductions and conclusions.

Source Text

The economic depression which spread over the world like a great conflagration toward the end of 1929 gave Adolf Hitler his opportunity. He made the most of it. A man like Hitler could thrive only during evil times—when the people were unemployed and desperate. Hitler was both ignorant of and uninterested in economics. But he was not uninterested in or ignorant of the opportunities which economic depression could provide. In the darkest days, when the factories were silent, when the registered unemployed numbered over six million and bread lines stretched for blocks in every city in the land, Hitler wrote in the Nazi press: "Never in my life have I been so well disposed and inwardly contented as in these days. For hard reality has opened the eyes of millions of Germans to the unprecedented swindles, lies and betrayals of the Marxist deceivers of the people." The suffering of his fellow Germans was not something to waste time sympathizing with, but rather to transform, cold-bloodedly and immediately, into political support for his own ambitions. Hitler successfully convinced those in power during the early 1930s that only he could rescue Germany from its disastrous economic predicament.

Parliamentary government was breaking down at the exact moment when the economic crisis made strong government imperative. New elections were called for—the hard-pressed people were demanding a way out of their sorry predicament. The millions of unemployed wanted jobs. The shopkeepers wanted help. Some four million youths who had come of voting age since the last election wanted some prospect of a future that would at least give them a living. To all the millions of discontented, Hitler, in a whirlwind campaign, offered what seemed to them, in their misery, some measure of hope. It was believed that he would make Germany strong again, stamp out corruption, and see to it that every German had a job. To hopeless people seeking not only relief but new faith and new gods, the appeal was not without effect.

Hitler's Minister of Economics made sure that Adolf had access to the wealthiest men in Germany. Hitler was highly skilled at telling these men of power, and people in general, what they wanted to hear. The Nazi party needed large sums of money to finance election campaigns, pay the bill for widespread and intensified propaganda, meet the payroll of hundreds of full-time officials, and maintain their private army. For example, Emil Kirdorf, the union-hating coal baron who presided over a political slush fund known as the "Ruhr Treasury," raised by mining interest, was seduced by Hitler during the party congress of 1929. Fritz Thyssen, the head of the steel trust, who lived to regret his folly and to write about it in a book titled *I Paid Hitler*, was an even bigger contributor.

By popular vote, Hitler was elected Chancellor of Germany in January of 1933. When he addressed the people one year later, in January 1934, he could look back on a year of achievement without parallel in German history. Within those twelve months he had overthrown the Weimar Republic, substituted his personal dictatorship for its democracy, destroyed all the political parties but his own, smashed the state governments and their parliaments and unified the Reich (Germany), wiped out the labor unions, stamped out democratic associations of every kind, driven the Jews out of public and professional life, abolished freedom of speech and of the press, stifled the independence of the courts and coordinated under Nazi rule the political, economic, cultural and social life of an ancient and cultivated people.

The Nazification of culture included establishment of the National Reich Church of Germany. Here are its central articles of establishment:
1) The National Reich Church of Germany categorically claims the exclusive right and the exclusive power to control all churches within the borders of the Reich. It declares these to be national churches of the German Reich.
2) The National Church is determined to exterminate irrevocably the strange and foreign Christian faiths imported into Germany in the ill-omened year 800.
3) The National church has no scribes, pastors, chaplains or priests, but National Reich orators are to speak in them.
4) The National Church demands immediate cessation of the publishing and dissemination of the Bible in Germany.
5) The National Church declares that to it, and therefore to the German nation, it has been decided that the Fuehrer's (Hitler's) *Mein Kampf* (autobiography) is the greatest of all documents. It not only contains the greatest but it embodies the purest and truest ethics for the present and future life of our nation.
6) The National Church will clear away from its altars all crucifixes, Bibles, and pictures of saints.
7) On the altars there must be nothing but *Mein Kampf* and to the left of the altar a sword.
8) The Christian Cross must be removed from all churches, cathedrals, and chapels, and it must be superseded by the only unconquerable symbol, the swastika.

Source: *The Rise and Fall of the Third Reich*
by William L. Shirer, 1960

Assignment
1. Read the source text to get a feeling about the mind and character of Adolf Hitler in the years leading up to the start of World War II.
2. Read at least one book or article about events leading up to, or during World War II. You can also use the Internet to research if you like. Decide what specific topics are most interesting to you. Focus your

imagination on those topics—imagine yourself being there. If you like, you can imagine yourself being a German citizen caught up in the economic and political events of the time.

3. Write a 5-paragraph composition including an introduction and a conclusion on what you imagine it was like. Follow the Structural Tools and Suggestions below. Be sure to include the style and structural elements for your level. Use the creative writing checksheet on page 92. Make an outline on a separate sheet of paper (following the model chart on page 91), and then write the rough draft. Edit and type a final copy as always. This is creative writing; have fun!

Structural Tools and Suggestions

1. Review the Creative Writing Procedure Chart on page 91. It is usually best to write the three body paragraphs first, and then write the introduction and conclusion based on what you have already written.
2. Be sure to include topic/clincher sentences in the body paragraphs, and to highlight (or bold) the topic key words in the introduction and conclusion as well.

Style Tools and Examples, (Levels B & C)

Triple "-ly" adverbs may be consecutive or spaced out, as in the following examples.

Consecutive

Adam **strongly**, **repeatedly**, and **consistently** confronted academia.

Spaced

Left destitute by the thousands, many World War II families **clearly** endured discrimination, **significantly** suffered a loss of wealth, and **ultimately** sacrificed their lives for a cause they believed in.

As a general rule, when putting three adverbs together, make sure they come from different categories on the accompanying chart. The three adverbs used in the first example above come from subsections I to III. Given the immense size of subsection VI, of course, three adverbs could easily be linked, as in:

She walked beautifully, calmly, and smoothly.
She walked calmly, smoothly, yet anxiously.
She walked calmly, dreamily, but somewhat proudly.

The words *yet* and *but* help when putting together three which normally do not go together.

Adverbs: "-ly" Words

I. Importance	II. Assurance	III. Frequency	IV. Sequence	V. Clincher Starters
entirely	assuredly	rapidly	AVOID:	clearly
significantly	presumably	frequently	firstly	assuredly
substantially	predictably	continuously	secondly	frequently
totally	fundamentally	immediately	thirdly	ultimately
increasingly	possibly	easily		obviously
essentially	probably	increasingly		undeniably
consistently	evidently	suddenly	CHOOSE:	gradually
primarily	undeniably	occasionally	initially	generally
customarily	readily	gently	eventually	usually
absolutely	normally	repeatedly	ultimately	normally
completely	clearly	quickly	originally	
virtually	willingly	normally	effectively	
seriously	surely	gradually	finally	
utterly	regularly	constantly	previously	
distinctly	rigidly	repeatedly		
notably	strictly	steadily		
	successfully			
	strongly			
	understandably			
	seriously			

VI. More Adverbs (Can you think of additional ones?)			
abnormally	enormously	loudly	willfully
abruptly	enticingly	madly	woefully
absentmindedly	entirely	marvelously	yearningly
absolutely	enviously	meaningfully	zealously
accusingly	especially	reluctantly	
actually	essentially	reassuringly	_____
adversely	evidently	regretfully	
amazingly	exactly	regularly	_____
angrily	excitedly	righteously	
anxiously	exclusively	rigidly	_____
arrogantly	expertly	scarcely	
assuredly	extremely	sedately	_____
awkwardly	fairly	seemingly	
badly	famously	sharply	_____
bashfully	fearlessly	sheepishly	
beautifully	fervently	sleepily	_____
briskly	foolishly	slyly	
calmly	freely	smoothly	_____
cheaply	frightfully	softly	
compassionately	gratefully	solidly	_____
confidently	greatly	speedily	*(cont.)*

crisply	hatefully	surprisingly	_____
crossly	heavily	suspiciously	
daintily	impulsively	truly	_____
delicately	intensely	undeniably	
determinedly	inwardly	vastly	_____
doggedly	lawfully	vehemently	
dreamily	longingly	vocally	_____

Lesson 18: The Key Terms of Economics

Objective
To further practice creative writing, including an introduction and a conclusion, following the steps in the previous two lessons.

Assignment
1. Refer to the chart of Key Terms listed on page 12 of this book. Select three of these terms for your use in this assignment.
2. Plan and write a 5-paragraph creative composition with an introduction, a 3-paragraph body, and a conclusion.
3. The themes (topics) of your 3-paragraph body are each of the three terms you have selected. Make sure these three work well together.
4. Use the facts you have already learned by looking up the definitions of the terms on page 12. You may now wish to do some additional reading on your selected terms. In addition, use your own imagination.
5. Remember to follow the process chart (below). Refer to the checksheet on page 101 to make sure you include all the necessary style and structural elements required of your level.

Step 1: Determine the subject.
Step 2: List possible topics. (in this case, from the chart on page 12)

_____	_____	_____
_____	_____	_____
_____	_____	_____

Step 3: Choose 3 topics; determine their order in the composition.
Step 4: Create an outline and details by taking "notes from your brain".
     Ask yourself questions about each topic.
Step 5: Write the body (topic) paragraphs.
Step 6: Write the introduction and conclusion paragraphs.

Style Tools and Examples
Accent, Level C
For the following words, if the accent is at the front of the word, it is a noun. If it is at the end, then it is a verb. Look at the word *refuse*. If the accent is 'ref-use, it is a noun referring to garbage, as in, "Put out the refuse since tomorrow is garbage day." When the accent comes at the end, re-'fuse, it is a verb, as in, "I refuse to do that." Study the following three examples on the next page, and then write sentences in the blanks provided for practice.

1. (Model)   'en-trance: Where is the entrance to the White House?
                   en-'trance: The bright new toys seemed to entrance the children.

2. (Model)   'pro-ceeds: They donated the proceeds from the banquet.
                   pro-'ceeds: After Dad leaves our home, he always proceeds to the office.

3. (Model)   'con-fines: Please remain within the confines of economic theory.
                   con-'fines: She confines the dog to the yard so he doesn't run off.

4. 'con-duct (n):_____

   con-'duct (v):_____

5. 'con-vict (n):_____

   con-'vict (v):_____

6. 'con-vert (n):_____

   con-'vert (v):_____

7. 'pres-ent (n):_____

   pres-'ent (v):_____

8. 'in-crease (n):_____

   in-'crease (v):_____

9. 'ob-ject (n):_____

   ob-'ject (v):_____

10. 'des-ert (n):_____

   de-'sert (v):_____

Checksheet for Lesson 18

Levels A, B, & C

Presentation
___ title centered and underlined
___ name, date
___ clearly presented

Mechanics
___ indent paragraphs
___ complete sentences
___ capitals (uppercase)
___ punctuation

Structure
___ follows model
___ paragraphs roughly equal size
___ topic and clincher sentences
(BODY PARAGRAPHS ONLY)
___ repeat or reflect 2–3 key words
___ title reflects key words of final sentence in Conclusion **or** last sentence of Introduction

Style Tools
___ underline dress-ups (one of each)
___ no "banned" adjectives
___ no "banned" verbs

Sentence Openers
___ ❶ subject
___ ❷ preposition
___ ❸ "-ly" word
___ ❹ "ing"/ "ed" opener
___ ❺ adverb clausal opener
___ ❻ VSS (<5 words)

Introduction   I.
Time, place, historical background ____
Three themes (topics) ____
Ends with title ____
Stylistic techniques at your level ____

Paragraphs	I.	II.	III.	IV.	V.

Level A

Dress-Ups

	I.	II.	III.	IV.	V.
"-ly" word	___	___	___	___	___
"who/which" clause	___	___	___	___	___
quality adjective	___	___	___	___	___
adverb clause (www.asia)	___	___	___	___	___
strong verb	___	___	___	___	___
Sentence Openers	___	___	___	___	___

Level B

Dress-Ups

	I.	II.	III.	IV.	V.
dual "-ly" words	___	___	___	___	___
"who/which" clause	___	___	___	___	___
invisible "who/which"	___	___	___	___	___
dual adjectives	___	___	___	___	___
adverbial clause	___	___	___	___	___
dual verb	___	___	___	___	___
Sentence Openers	___	___	___	___	___
Decoration	___	___	___	___	___

Level C

Dress-Ups

	I.	II.	III.	IV.	V.
dual "-ly" word	___	___	___	___	___
"who/which" clause	___	___	___	___	___
invisible "who/which"	___	___	___	___	___
adj. "teeter-totter"	___	___	___	___	___
adverbial clause	___	___	___	___	___
dual verbs	___	___	___	___	___
Sentence Openers	___	___	___	___	___
Decoration	___	___	___	___	___
Triple "-ly" Adverbs	___	___	___	___	___

Conclusion   V.
Repeats three themes (topics) ____
Most important? Why? ____
Least important? Why? ____
Stylistic techniques (at your level) ____

Unit VIII: Essay Composition
Lesson 19: Three Views of Poverty Revisited

Objective
To study the fundamentals of essay writing by revising and expanding a previously written report. This lesson provides an assignment with the basic essay form, which should suffice for students of all levels, however if students require a more difficult and sophisticated level of essay writing, please proceed to the super-essay format found in the *Teaching Writing: Structure & Style* seminar.

Source Text

Poverty is a matter not so much of low incomes but of how people cope with the fact of having low incomes. Some low-income households honestly, industriously, and successfully make do with what they have, keep families together, and keep children out of trouble. Others, including many that statistically speaking have been raised above the so called poverty threshold, are for one reason or another unable to cope. They fall into a pattern of social pathologies ranging from juvenile crime and teenage pregnancy to drug and alcohol abuse. They turn newly constructed public housing into instant slums, and in a variety of ways they frustrate the hopes of those who aspire to eliminate poverty through generous public spending and giving. *(cont. next page col. 1)*	The wealthiest 1 percent of the population owns over 40 percent of all capital. The wealthiest 20 percent of U.S. citizens earn over 40 percent of all personal income, while the poorest 20 percent must make do with only 5 percent of the total. Behind these simple statistics lies a whole host of economic policy issues. In the United States today, it is widely accepted that one of the major functions of government is to influence the distribution of income. There is no doubt that poverty exists in the United States despite the fact that its people, by many measures, continue to have the highest average incomes in the world. Poverty is plainly seen in vast neighborhoods in every large city. It is tucked away only slightly less visibly in small towns and *(cont. next page col. 2)*	What constitutes low income must be defined in subjective terms, relative to the incomes of others in society. A poverty-level household income should be defined as one equal to less than half of the median income for all households in a given society. So, poverty-level income is really a moving target rather than an objectively defined threshold. Nonetheless, poverty can be overcome by raising the incomes of the poor in proper proportion to the incomes of everybody else in a given society. The reason our government selected an objective, need-based official definition of poverty in the first place was to provide a benchmark against which to measure progress toward the elimination of poverty. On the basis of the official definition, the incidence of poverty fell *(cont. next page col. 3)*

No amount of income redistribution can by itself eliminate poverty. If poorly conceived government programs foster dependency and destroy self-respect, they make things worse. They, in fact, foster the continuance of the cycle of poverty. Efforts to redistribute income are reflected not only in explicit anti-poverty programs but also in the tendency to subject almost every policy decision to the test: What does it do for the poor?

Perhaps, we might do more for the poor by helping the entrepreneur, the small businessman, and by assisting the creative and innovative forces at work in our economy. These are the engines that drive the future. These are the people who build wealth for our nation. Jobs are created for the jobless, and charitable donations are made possible through an increase in the success rate of small business ventures.

rural areas throughout our country. People are poor if they cannot afford the simple necessities of life—food, clothing, and shelter.

With government programs, we can raise people up out of poverty by lifting their incomes above an objectively defined poverty threshold. This is the official view of the United States government—and for good reason. This approach begins with the idea of an "economy food plan" devised by the U.S. Department of Agriculture*. The plan calculates the cost of providing a balanced nutritive diet. The cost of the plan varies according to the size of a given family, the age of its members, and their place of residence. Other needs must be satisfied too, so, to take those other needs into account, the government sets the low-income level—the dividing line between the poor and the non-poor— at three times the cost of the "economy food plan."
*USDA – CNPP (Thrifty Food Plan)

rapidly during the 1960s—from 22.4 percent of the population in 1959 to 12.1 percent in 1969. During the 1970s, 1980s, 1990s, and in the new millennium, there has been essentially no further reduction in the number of officially measured poor families. In fact, certain measurements indicate that the percentages are returning now to the pre-1960s era. Therefore, the government must do something with great haste and effort!

The officially defined poverty threshold is not enough. It is time for subjective reasoning to play a part. Objective measurements are only useful to a point. It is imperative to realize that the wealthiest 1 percent of the population owns over 40 percent of all capital, and the wealthiest 20 percent of U.S. citizens earn over 40 percent of all personal income, while the poorest 20 percent must make do with only 5 percent of the total. It is time for aggressive, government-directed redistribution!

Assignment

1. Find your completed 3-paragraph report on Three Views of Poverty from Lesson 11. This will provide the body for your essay. Edit and rewrite these three paragraphs using your newer, more advanced stylistic techniques. You will see how much you have learned!
2. Consider what type of background information would fit nicely to form the introduction, as well as what might be seen as the most significant idea to focus on in the conclusion.
3. Research a little to find additional references or commentaries on the subject of poverty. Use these to embellish your writing for this assignment.

Structure & Style Tools and Suggestions

One significant difference between a "report" and an "essay" is that in an essay you must analyze the facts or details rather than just state them. The conclusion is the critical element of an essay and should include your opinion or original ideas, although it is important to avoid using "I think..." or "In my opinion..." statements. Your conclusion must state what is the most important or significant topic or aspect of a topic.

Before writing, and as part of your preparation, search for other sources. If you have access to a library or online resources, you will find many references on the economic problem of poverty—take some notes, remembering the specific topic of "Poverty." Focus your search toward finding topics which could potentially answer the main question. Ultimately, in an essay, you must give your own opinion as to which theory or theme seems most convincing to you. Find support for your theory/theme in order to strengthen your essay.

Advanced students may want to take this opportunity to write a significantly more in-depth analysis of the economic and political realities surrounding the subject of poverty, and discuss more than five themes. In that case, one of the following super-essay models would provide a way to organize a multitude of topics. As is evident from the diagram on the next page, a super-essay consists of two (or three) Basic (or Extended) essays on related subjects glued together with a super-introduction and a super-conclusion. In such a case, much more commentary and depth of analysis is required.

Advanced students should refer to their MLA Handbook for the proper formatting of a bibliography and handling of quotations and footnotes.

THE SUPER-ESSAY MODEL	THE SUPER-DUPER ESSAY MODEL
I. SUPER-INTRODUCTION II. Introduction – Essay One III. Topic A IV. Topic B V. Topic C VI. Conclusion – Essay One VII. Introduction – Essay Two VIII. Topic D IX. Topic E X. Topic F XI. Conclusion – Essay Two XII. SUPER-CONCLUSION	I. SUPER-INTRODUCTION II. Introduction – Essay One III. Topic A IV. Topic B V. Topic C VI. Conclusion – Essay One VII. Introduction – Essay Two VIII. Topic D IX. Topic E X. Topic F XI. Topic G XII. Conclusion – Essay Two XIII. Introduction – Essay Three XIV. Topic H XV. Topic I XVI. Topic J XVII. Topic K XVIII. Conclusion – Essay Three XIX. SUPER-CONCLUSION

Checksheet for Lesson 19

Levels A, B, & C

Presentation
___ title centered and underlined
___ name, date
___ clearly presented
___ space between paragraphs

Mechanics
___ indent paragraphs
___ complete sentences
___ capitals (uppercase)
___ punctuation

Structure
___ follows model
___ paragraphs roughly equal size
___ topic and clincher sentences
(BODY PARAGRAPHS ONLY)
___ repeat or reflect 2–3 key words
___ title reflects key words of final sentence in Conclusion **or** last sentence of Introduction

Style Tools
___ underline dress-ups (one of each)
___ no "banned" adjectives
___ no "banned" verbs

Sentence Openers
___ ❶ subject
___ ❷ preposition
___ ❸ "-ly" word
___ ❹ "ing"/"ed" opener
___ ❺ adverb clausal opener
___ ❻ VSS (<5 words)

Introduction   I.

setting/historical background   ____
states three topics   ____
poses a question   ____
dress-up   ____
sentence openers   ____
decoration (B&C)   ____
triple "-ly" adverbs (C)   ____

Body Paragraphs	II.	III.	IV.
topic/clincher related	____	____	____
dress up	____	____	____
sentence openers	____	____	____
decoration (B&C)	____	____	____
triple "-ly" adverbs (B&C)	____	____	____
strong verb	____	____	____

Conclusion   V.

repeats three themes (topics)   ____
most important? Why?   ____
answers question   ____
dress-up   ____
sentence openers   ____
decoration (B&C)   ____
triple "-ly" adverbs (C)   ____

Note: Please customize this checklist for each student by crossing off techniques not understood. This page may be photocopied for use with future essays.

Lesson 20: Communism vs. Capitalism

Objective
To further practice essay writing, utilizing the Super-Essay Model.

Assignment
1. Research Communism and Capitalism isolating several key facts pertaining to each of these highly diverse economic systems.
2. Plan and write a 5-paragraph essay on Communism.
3. Plan and write a 5-paragraph essay on Capitalism.
4. Merge the two essays together comparing and contrasting with the addition of a super-introduction and a super-conclusion.
5. Make sure the themes (topics) of your 3-paragraph bodies work well together in support of the overall theme you find most important. Select the same three themes for each sub-essay so that when you compare and contrast, a direct correlation may be easily drawn.
6. In structuring your super-conclusion you must carefully analyze the facts you have gathered through your research. In addition, use your own imagination. Decide how your conclusion will be structured— judge for yourself which are the most important aspects. Find support for your chosen theory/theme in order to strengthen your essay.
7. Remember to follow the Super-Essay Model outlined on page 106. Refer to the page 110 checksheet for Lessons 20 and 21 to make sure you include all the necessary style and structural elements required of your level.

Source Texts
There is no single source text provided for this assignment. Rather, you are expected to research relevant subject matter on your own, taking notes and formulating arguments for your super-essay comparing and contrasting Communism and Capitalism. Below, I have provided several references from my own library to get you started. You can find these references at Google Books online or at your local public library. Feel free to use online dictionaries and encyclopedias. You may also find several critical essays available on the Internet.

Communism

Marx, Karl (1886) *Capital: A Critical Analysis of Capitalist Production.*

Conquest, Robert (2000) *Reflections on a Ravaged Century.*

Forman, James D. (1972) *Communism from Marx's Manifesto to 20th century Reality.*

Daniels, Robert V. (1994) *A Documentary History of Communism and the World: From Revolution to Collapse.*

Dirlik, Arif (1989) *Origins of Chinese Communism.*

"Communism" *The Columbia Encyclopedia* (6th ed.). 2007.

"Communism" *Merriam-Webster Online Dictionary.* Merriam-Webster Online. 2009. http://www.merriam-webster.com/dictionary/communism

"Communism" *Encyclopædia Britannica* 2006. Encyclopædia Britannica Online.

Capitalism

Wood, Ellen Meiksins (2002) *The Origins of Capitalism: A Longer View.*

Obrinsky, Mark (1983) *Profit Theory and Capitalism.*

Lash, Scott and Urry, John (2000) *Capitalism.*

Bacher, Christian (2007) *Capitalism, Ethics and the Paradoxon of Self-exploitation.*

Bottomore, Tom (1985) *Theories of Modern Capitalism.*

Friedman, Milton (1952) *Capitalism and Freedom.*

Galbraith, J.K. (1952) *American Capitalism.*

Heilbroner, Robert L. (1966) *The Limits of American Capitalism.*

Reisman, George (1996) *Capitalism: A Treatise on Economics.*

Weber, Max (1926) *The Protestant Ethic and the Spirit of Capitalism.*

Checksheet for Lessons 20 & 21

Levels A, B, & C

Presentation
___ title centered and underlined
___ name, date
___ clearly presented
___ space between paragraphs

Mechanics
___ indent paragraphs
___ complete sentences
___ capitals (uppercase)
___ punctuation

Structure
___ follows model
___ paragraphs roughly equal size
___ topic and clincher sentences
(BODY PARAGRAPHS ONLY)
___ repeat or reflect 2-3 key words
___ title reflects key words of final sentence in Conclusion **or** last sentence of Introduction

Style Tools
___ underline dress-ups (one of each)
___ no "banned" adjectives
___ no "banned" verbs

Sentence Openers
___ ❶ subject
___ ❷ preposition
___ ❸ "-ly" word
___ ❹ "ing"/"ed" opener
___ ❺ adverb clausal opener
___ ❻ VSS (<5 words)

Essay 1 Introduction & Essay 2 Introduction	I.	II.
setting/historical background	___	___
states three topics	___	___
poses a question	___	___
dress-up	___	___
sentence openers	___	___
decoration (B&C)	___	___
triple "-ly" adverbs (C)	___	___

Body Paragraphs	III.	IV.	V.	VI.	VII.	VIII.
topic/clincher related	___	___	___	___	___	___
dress up	___	___	___	___	___	___
sentence openers	___	___	___	___	___	___
decoration (B&C)	___	___	___	___	___	___
triple "-ly" adverbs	___	___	___	___	___	___
strong verb	___	___	___	___	___	___

Essay 1 Conclusion & Essay 2 Conclusion	IX.	X.
repeats three themes (topics)	___	___
most important? Why?	___	___
answers question	___	___
dress-up	___	___
sentence openers	___	___
decoration (B&C)	___	___
triple "-ly" adverbs (C)	___	___

Note: Please customize this checklist for each student by crossing off techniques not understood. This page may be photocopied for use with future essays. The super-introduction and super-conclusion paragraphs are in addition to the ten paragraphs charted in this checksheet. These should recapitulate and strengthen the underlying introductions and conclusions.

Lesson 21: Socialism vs. Distributism

Objective
To further practice essay writing, utilizing the Super-Essay Model.

Assignment
1. Research Socialism and Distributism, isolating several key facts pertaining to each of these economic systems.
2. Plan and write a 5-paragraph essay on Socialism.
3. Plan and write a 5-paragraph essay on Distributism.
4. Merge the two essays together comparing and contrasting with the addition of a super-introduction and a super-conclusion.
5. Make sure the themes (topics) of your 3-paragraph bodies work well together in support of the overall theme you find most important. Select the same three themes for each sub-essay so that when you compare and contrast, a direct correlation may be easily drawn.
6. In structuring your super-conclusion you must carefully analyze the facts you have gathered through your research. In addition, use your own imagination. Decide how your conclusion will be structured— judge for yourself which are the most important aspects. Find support for your chosen theory/theme in order to strengthen your essay.
7. Remember to follow the Super-Essay Model outlined on page 106. Refer to the page 110 checksheet for Lessons 20 and 21 to make sure you include all the necessary style and structural elements required of your level.

Source Texts
There is no single source text provided for this assignment. Rather, you are expected to research relevant subject matter on your own, taking notes and formulating arguments for your super-essay comparing and contrasting Socialism and Distributism. Below, I have provided several references from my own library to get you started. You can find these references at Google Books online or at your local public library. Also, I have provided one online address to a critical essay on Distributism. You may find several additional critical essays available on the Internet.

Socialism

Muravchik, Joshua (1995) *Heaven on Earth: The Rise and Fall of Socialism.*

Engels, Friedrich (1989) *Socialism: Utopian and Scientific.*

Fried, Albert and Sanders, Ronald (1964) *Socialist Thought: A Documentary History.*

Itoh, Makoto (1995) *Political Economy of Socialism.*

Weinstein, James (2003) *Long Detour: The History and Future of the American Left.*

Von Mises, Ludwig (1922) *Socialism: An Economic and Sociological Analysis.*

Newman, Michael (2005) *Socialism: A Very Short Introduction.*

Ollman, Bertell (1998) *Market Socialism: The Debate among Socialists.*

Distributism

Chesterton, G. K. (1921) *The Uses of Diversity.*

Belloc, Hilaire (1913) *The Servile State.*

Cooney, Anthony (2001) *Distributism.*

Sagar, S. (1940) *Distributism.*

"Essay on Distributism" (2007) British Nationalist Party online
http://web.archive.org/web/20071016030401/www.bnp.org.uk/articles/deadly_twins1.htm

Critique Vocabulary Thesaurus

The thesaurus below provides alternatives to words that you might overuse when you write critiques. The synonyms are arranged according to the paragraph where you might need them. As you will see in the next unit, you can use any of the synonyms below to replace less descriptive options. Not all of the words can be used interchangeably, so you must learn the terms and know when to use each one. The exercise that follows the thesaurus will help develop your knowledge of these terms.

Introduction

Story tale, saga, narrative, epic, legend, mystery, tragedy, comedy, romance, novel, yarn, anecdote, myth

Type sad, nature, science fiction, love, adventure, historical, horror, folk, fairy, animal, moral, space, descriptive

Characters
(players, actors, heroes, personae, participants, figures, villain, victim)

Role main, central, leading, major, minor, subordinate, lesser, supporting, shadowy, background, secondary

Type adventurous, tragic, comic, bumbling, retiring, extroverted, pliant, scheming, sordid, acquisitive, inquisitive, impulsive, sinister

Analysis well- or poorly-drawn, convincing, fully or underdeveloped, consistent, lifeless, too perfect, overly evil, idyllic

Setting

Time long ago, ancient, Medieval, modern, contemporary, futuristic, mythical

Place rural, urban, small town, frontier, pioneer, war, space, slums, ghetto, exotic, foreign land

Mood mysterious, foreboding, tragic, bland, comic, violent, suspenseful, compelling, sad, supernatural, emotional

Conflict/Plot

(plan, conspiracy, scheme, intrigue, subplot, sequence of events, action, narrative, episode)

Stages   initiated, promoted, continued, expanded, resolved

Intensity   exacerbated, heightened, lessened

Analysis   over or underplayed, realistic, unrealistic, convincing, contrived, stretched, sketchy

Climax   turning point, most exciting moment, dramatic event, high point, crisis, anticlimactic, inevitable, conclusion

Analysis

Theme   message, moral, lesson, topic, subtheme, matter, subject

Techniques foreshadowing, symbolism, quality of language, short sentences, repetition, relation of subplot to the narrative

****

Thesaurus Assignment

1. Using the Critique Vocabulary Thesaurus and a dictionary if needed, fill in the most appropriate words for the following:

    a. A long involved story of heroic achievements such as the Icelandic prose narrative - _____

    b. A true or fictitious narrative - _____

    c. A written account of connected events in order of happening - _____

    d. A long story with heroic figures, large crowds and events, relative and whole nations - _____

    e. A traditional narrative usually involving supernatural or imaginary persons - _____

    f. A short account of an interesting or entertaining incident - _____

    g. An incredible, usually magical story - _____

h. A fiction based on technological advances, frequently portraying time travel or life on other planets - _____

i. A book where fictitious persons are blended into actual historical events - _____

2. Give four synonyms for each of the following, using words from the thesaurus.

    a. participants _____

    b. scheme of events _____

    c. subject matter _____

    d. foreboding _____

    e. emotional crisis _____

3. List three stages in the development of the conflict:

    _____

4. List three literary devices or techniques:

    _____

5. What literary technique is used to:

    a. hint at future events? _____

    b. give emphasis? _____

    c. use one thing to hint at another? _____

    d. startle the reader? _____

Unit IX: Writing Reviews or Critiques
Lesson 22: We'll Stash Your Trash in a Flash, Again!

Objective
To begin writing critiques which follow the 3-paragraph model demonstrated in Unit III but add an introduction and conclusion.

Source Text

Brian Scudamore started his company 1-800-GOT-JUNK? in 1989 straight out of high school with $700 and a beat-up old pick-up truck. Today they have over 300 franchise partners across North America with a true national presence—they are in 47 of North America's top 50 cities. Scudamore was a risk-taker, but firm in his vision. "With a vision of creating the 'FedEx' of junk removal," says Scudamore, "I dropped out of University with just one year left to become a fulltime JUNKMAN! Yes, my father, a liver transplant surgeon, was not impressed to say the least."

Many entrepreneurs minimize their risks by outsourcing to contractors. Scudamore chose a different route. "I hired my first employee a week after I started. I knew I needed the help. His name was David Sniderman—a good friend of mine. I really didn't know yet how to hire so I just asked a buddy." It may have started as a matter of simply not knowing what else to do, but it became a philosophical issue for him. "I always believed in hiring people. I felt that if I wasn't willing to make the investment then I was questioning my own faith in the business." On the other hand, he's a big believer in letting other people share some of the risk. His choice of franchising as a business model allowed him rapid growth without having to turn to outside investors or other funding sources. "It's the ultimate leverage model. People pay you a fee up-front to help them grow. Rather than lose control of my vision by going public—I chose franchising." Brian has managed to retain 100% ownership and bootstrapped the business solely out of cash flow—something that is very rare these days.

Although this is a simple business, they couldn't possibly have grown this quickly without technology. Taking a low tech business and putting a high tech spin on it allowed them to rapidly distinguish themselves from their competition. All calls come into a central 1-800-GOT-JUNK? call center where they do all the booking and dispatch for their franchise partners. Franchise partners then assess all of their real time reports, schedules, customer info, etc., off of JUNKNET, their corporate intranet. This allows franchise partners to get into business quickly, and to focus solely on growth.

1-800-GOT-JUNK? did over $35 Million in sales during their fiscal year 2005— not a bad return on a $700.00 investment! The company continues to grow year-after-year, building themselves into the world's largest junk removal service—

now going international.

This single-page article was originally written in 2004 by Scott Allen, a 20-year veteran technology entrepreneur, executive, consultant, and "Entrepreneurs Guide" for About.com, one of the top ten websites in the world with over 37 million readers, and a subsidiary of the *New York Times*. Scott offers current and future entrepreneurs guidance and resources to help them start and develop their new businesses. Article reprinted and updated with permission.

Assignment
1. Reread the source text. This is the same source text that you began to critique in Lesson 6. Revisit the outline you created using the Narrative Story Model for the three body paragraphs in Lesson 6.
2. Use the tools below to outline the introduction and conclusion you will now be adding.
3. Finally, rewrite your own critique, adding the new elements you have learned since Lesson 6 to the three body paragraphs. Also, add your new introduction and conclusion paragraphs.

Structural Tools and Suggestions
Find and follow your story sequence model in Lesson 6. The objective of this present lesson is to take a story summary and expand it into a more objective review, or simple critique.

Introductions
In general, critique introductions must include certain necessary pieces of information. You may include additional information as well, but the following are the required elements:

1. Story, book, speech, video, article or other title
2. Author, and short biographical information
3. Date or year of first publication or first presentation
4. Number of pages, length of presentation
5. Pictures (if any) – number and quality

Conclusions
Critique conclusions should include your opinions about what was strong or weak in the story, book, speech, video or other presentation and why, what you liked best and least and why. The conclusion should generally include the following:

1. Likes and strengths. Why?
2. Dislikes and weaknesses. Why?
3. Overall meaning and value of the story, book, speech or video.
4. Words reflecting the title (at end of the paragraph).

The "why" commentary is crucial because it provides the reader with what you believe to be the most important point of the story, book, speech or video. Again, however, avoid using the word *I* and expressions such as "I think..." and "I believe..."

Checksheet for Critiques - Lessons 22 & 23

Presentation
____ title centered and underlined
____ name, date
____ clearly presented
____ space between paragraphs
____ no banned words
____ underline dress-ups

Mechanics
____ indent paragraphs
____ complete sentences
____ punctuation

Structure
____ follows model
____ paragraphs roughly equal size
____ title reflects final sentence of first paragraph and/or last paragraph

Sentence Openers
____ ❶ subject
____ ❷ preposition
____ ❸ "-ly" word
____ ❹ "ing"/"ed" opener
____ ❺ adverb clausal opener
____ ❻ VSS (<5 words)

Introduction	I.
story/book/speech/video title	____
author's name	____
publication information	____
number of pages, etc.	____
dress-up	____
sentence openers	____
decoration	____
triple "-ly" adverbs	____

Body Paragraphs	II.	III.	IV.
dress up	____	____	____
sentence openers	____	____	____
decoration	____	____	____
triple "-ly" adverbs	____	____	____

Conclusion	V.
liked/strengths, why?	____
disliked/weaknesses, why?	____
value, significance, why?	____
dress-up	____
sentence openers	____
decoration	____
triple "-ly" adverbs	____

Note: Please customize this checklist for each student by crossing off techniques not understood. This page should be photocopied for use with future critiques.

Lesson 23: Economic Recovery
Excerpt from a speech by
Vice Chairman Donald L. Kohn, United States Federal Reserve.
Presented at the Hutchinson Lecture, Newark, Delaware
on April 20, 2009
(1-hour presentation)

Objective
To practice critique writing.

Source Text

Consideration of the likely shape of the recovery depends very much on understanding how we got to where we are now. For a number of years earlier in the decade, U.S. economic growth was supported importantly by rapid increases in consumption and housing, which, in turn, were fueled by an extended surge of global credit. Housing demand was propelled, in part, by persistently low long-term interest rates, loose underwriting standards on mortgages, and, for a while, expectations of continuing increases in house prices that resulted in the building of too many houses and the elevation of home prices to unsustainable levels. These same developments fed a surge in consumption through the effects on wealth of rising house prices and through various financial innovations that allowed many households to liquefy their housing wealth. Financial intermediaries were further exposed by generally inadequate compensation for risk and increased leverage. As the housing boom petered out and then reversed, both households and lenders found themselves overextended, developments that led to a mutually reinforcing pullback in spending and lending. The dynamics of this adjustment, which coincided with the collapse of the global credit boom, helped push the U.S. economy into deep recession.

Along with its monetary policy actions, the Federal Reserve has been part of a broader government effort—one that includes the Treasury and the Federal Deposit Insurance Corporation (FDIC)—to provide more direct support to financial firms and the economy. In part, this effort has involved targeted actions to prevent the failure or substantial weakening of specific systemically important institutions when the disorderly failure of a large, complex, interconnected firm would disrupt the functioning of a range of financial markets and impede the flow of credit to households and businesses. Besides this targeted support, the government has been injecting capital into the banking system to ensure that U.S. banking institutions are well capitalized and can support the recovery by lending to sound households and businesses. In addition to the programs to provide capital, the government, through the FDIC, has temporarily guaranteed selected liabilities of insured depository institutions and their holding companies, thereby improving their access to funding. The government has also taken steps, most recently through the Making Home Affordable program, to reduce unnecessary foreclosures. Beyond helping homeowners stay in their houses, limiting foreclosures should benefit lenders, mitigate adverse impacts on affected communities, and, by limiting the decline in overall home prices, help support the broader economy. Finally, the Treasury recently announced a program to assist banks and other lenders in finding markets for their "legacy assets"—that is, real estate-related assets that were accumulated during the housing boom and have since declined in value and become relatively illiquid. Uncertainty about the value of legacy assets is weighing on confidence in banks, and so helping banks to dispose of such assets should contribute to their ability to raise capital and increase lending.

Employing its fiscal policy tools, the government has enacted a multifaceted program of stimulus that will provide direct support to spending and economic activity. In February, the President signed into law a $787 billion package that included cuts in taxes and increases in transfer payments for households, lower taxes for businesses, higher spending for infrastructure investments, and additional financial assistance to state and local governments, many of which would otherwise have been forced to cut spending in response to declining revenues. Although the exact effects of these measures on the economy are difficult to gauge, they will likely provide a significant boost to activity. According to the Congressional Budget Office, the effect of the stimulus package on the level of real GDP at the end of 2010 could range from about 1 percent to more than 3 percent, relative to a baseline forecast that does not include the stimulus. That additional GDP translates into an unemployment rate by the end of next year that is between 1/2 and 2 percentage points lower than it otherwise would be. With the tax cuts already showing up in paychecks, increases in transfer payments already in place, and grants to states and localities starting to flow, the effects of the package on aggregate demand should start to provide some support to activity fairly quickly.

The path of the economy will depend critically on how quickly the current stresses in financial markets abate; these events have few if any precedents, and thus it is very difficult to predict how the adjustment process will play out. But at the end of the process, our financial system will be on firmer footing. Both markets and regulators will continue to press financial firms to employ less leverage and have more reliable sources of liquidity, and those firms will have every incentive to more effectively price, monitor, and manage risk. Improvements to the supervisory and regulatory framework will help create a more stable financial system. In addition, we will have a stronger economy. Businesses will have boosted the efficiency of their operations. And households will be less indebted and saving more. That greater saving will, all else being equal, support greater investment or allow domestic saving to displace foreign saving for a more sustainable international position. The U.S. economy has proven itself over the years to be flexible and resilient as well as innovative and productive, qualities that enable it to rebound from serious economic shocks, and I am confident that, in a like manner, we will rebound from our current economic and financial challenges.

Dr. Kohn was born in November 1942 in Philadelphia, Pennsylvania. He received a B.A. in Economics in 1964 from the College of Wooster and a Ph.D. in Economics in 1971 from the University of Michigan. On June 23, 2006, Dr. Kohn was sworn in as Vice Chairman of the Board of Governors of the Federal Reserve System for a four-year term ending June 23, 2010.

Assignment
Write a critique of this speech excerpt. If you happen to be writing your critique long after the date this speech was delivered, then it will be fun to see how accurate Dr. Kohn was in his forecasting. Then you will be critiquing an historical event just as you might critique a speech delivered by Abraham Lincoln.

Follow the checksheet on page 119.

Style Tools and Examples
Practice using triple clauses in your compositions. For instance,

> What was Vice Chairman Kohn doing? Three things – explaining, justifying, encouraging.

Now construct a sentence with triple clauses:

> *Vice Chairman Kohn has been successful because he knows how to explain a complex situation, because he is gifted at justifying governmental actions, and because he is resolved to encourage others with his vision of recovery.*

Using the following phrases and words (or variants of them), create sentences with triple clauses.

1. Why did Adam Smith write *The Wealth of Nations*? (explaining, interacting, benefiting)

(because)_____

_____

_____

_____

2. Why did the Dutch become fascinated with tulips? (symbols, leveraging, wealth)

(because)_____

_____

_____

_____

3. Why did Brian Scudamore want to use technology? (differentiate, control, respond quickly)

(because)_____

_____

_____

_____

Congratulations!

You have finished the 23 economics-based writing lessons in this book. Undoubtedly, you have improved your writing skills, but hopefully you have also learned to think a bit more about innovation, entrepreneurialism, business plans, your freedom, politics, the economy, and the world around you.

You also have completed lessons from all nine units of the *Teaching Writing: Structure & Style* syllabus, and should now be able to design your own writing projects using any source of information. Although you probably have your style checklist memorized by now, you might like to remove some of the checksheets, charts, and lists from this book and keep them in a notebook for future reference.

I sincerely hope that you have experienced a process of writing practice, reading, critical thinking, contemplation, and dedication to freedomship that will continue throughout your life.

About the Author

Daniel Weber holds an M.B.A. from Pepperdine University as well as an M.P.S. (Pastoral Studies) from Loyola University. He has had published a wide range of academic articles, including ones covering innovation, entrepreneurialism, stewardship, and spirituality. Daniel is an innovator and inventor himself, holding four U.S. patents. He worked in high-tech international business management from 1981–2001, and taught international business management at Cal Poly from 2002–2006.

Today, his friends say he moved from high-tech to "higher-tech" because Daniel is also an ordained minister. He serves as chaplain at a maximum security state hospital in California.